D0507844

C333661116

A German
Tommy

God hath given you one face, and you make yourselves another.

William Shakespeare, *Hamlet*, Act 3 scene 1

A German Tommy

The Secret of a War Hero

Ken Anderson

Pen & Sword
MILITARY

First published in Great Britain in 2014 by
Pen & Sword Military
an imprint of
Pen & Sword Books Ltd
47 Church Street
Barnsley
South Yorkshire
S70 2AS

ISBN 978 1 78346 274 2

A CIP catalogue record for this book is available from the British
Library

Typeset in Ehrhardt by
Mac Style, Driffield, East Yorkshire
Printed and bound in the UK by CPI Group (UK) Ltd, Croydon,
CRO 4YY

Pen & Sword Books Ltd incorporates the imprints of Pen & Sword
Archaeology, Atlas, Aviation, Battleground, Discovery, Family
History, History, Maritime, Military, Naval, Politics, Railways,
Select, Transport, True Crime, and Fiction, Frontline Books, Leo
Cooper, Praetorian Press, Seaforth Publishing and Wharncliffe.

For a complete list of Pen & Sword titles please contact
PEN & SWORD BOOKS LIMITED
47 Church Street, Barnsley, South Yorkshire, S70 2AS, England
E-mail: enquiries@pen-and-sword.co.uk
Website: www.pen-and-sword.co.uk

Contents

Acknowledgements

My thanks must first go to Linne Matthews for her competent and conscientious editing of the final manuscript. Further thanks to Carl Harrison-Ford for his constructive critique of an earlier draft; to Peter and Lydia Anderson for their critical help during the work in progress; to fellow author Michael Foley for his encouragement and generosity; to Jonathan Wright, Lisa Hooson and others at Pen and Sword who saw the story's potential; to researchers Chris Baker in the United Kingdom and Jeanette Finlayson in Toowoomba, Queensland; and to staff at various libraries and records offices in Australia and Britain who willingly responded to my often complex inquiries. I also acknowledge the help of relatives of the gallant men mentioned herein, including relatives of Walter Schwarz (alias Lieutenant Walter Lancelot Merritt MC and Bar), Joyce Hampson and Mrs Betty Bradley, members of Senator Mattner's family, including Margaret Crisp, Barbara Hughes, Katherine Daniell and Charles Mattner, and Mrs Mary Thiele, daughter-in-law of Herbert Thiele, one of the three young brothers who were First World War volunteers. Finally, a thank you to my wife, Jacqueline, who had to put up with my 'occasional' outbursts of frustration brought on by the creation of *A German Tommy*.

Preliminary Notes

Quotes attributed to Walter Schwarz are taken throughout from his petition to King George V unless otherwise stated. Some accounts show his name as 'Schwartz' and/or the middle name as 'Lesley'. Throughout I use the name shown on his birth certificate: Walter Leslie Schwarz.

It has been impossible to determine if any copyright is attached to some of the illustrations in this book. Any infringement of copyright as a result of their publication is entirely unintentional; if any copyright has been infringed, the author extends his apologies to the parties concerned.

Introduction

The date: 14 October 1918, a foggy early morning, east of Ledeghem, Belgium. Young British Army officer Lieutenant Walter Lancelot Merritt carries a large red flag to indicate the centre of a brigade-strength advance. He moves ahead of the main force. Close to the German lines a bullet smashes into his right leg. Despite the crippling wound he continues to hold the flag aloft, ensuring following troops maintain the line as they move on to take long-entrenched German territory. Merritt's courage and leadership resulted in the award of a Bar to his Military Cross.

While undergoing treatment in post-war England, he confessed in a petition to King George his real name was Walter Schwarz. He had deserted from the Australian Imperial Force (AIF) in 1915 because he feared his German ancestry would prevent him being sent into battle. Within days he had joined a high-profile unit, the Sportsman's Battalion, under his assumed name and claiming to be the son of an Englishman. Records show these and other false claims in his official service records were accepted without question. George, who had personally decorated him as Merritt at Buckingham Palace, granted him a rare royal pardon, acting on advice from military and political advisers in Britain and Australia.

The mystery has remained to this day: how did Schwarz manage to maintain his cover for six long years under the most trying circumstances imaginable? Schwarz's only comment was he would like to say more but could not. He never did. Through research in Australia and Britain I have managed to go beyond what have been for nearly a century the officially accepted facts of this story to reveal for the first time the truth of this gallant deserter's incredible adventure. Had he died on the battlefield, this story would have been concealed forever. My research has led me to conclude that members of a secret society helped him maintain his cover while advancing what he most wanted in life – a long military career. This is a story of bravery and deception, unique in the history of war.

Other related chapters include the revelation that British soldiers of German ancestry, including decorated, wounded and long-serving men, were pulled out of the fighting and drafted into a non-combatants' battalion. A contemporary British historian at first denied such a battalion had existed until shown the proof.

Ken Anderson, 2013

Chapter 1

'A Deserving Class of People'

Captain Arthur Phillip and Augustus Theodore Alt were the first persons of German origin to set foot on Australian soil. Phillip landed at Sydney Cove on 26 January 1788 to found, and then govern, the British colony of New South Wales (NSW). The son of a language teacher who had migrated to Britain from Frankfurt, he was born in London in 1738 (died 1814). Alt (1731–1815) arrived with him as the first Surveyor-General of the colony. Born in England, he was the son of Justice Heinrich Alt, ambassador for Hesse-Kassel, and his English wife Jeanetta.

Germans were to become the first ethnic minority to form a cultural community in Australia. Picturesque villages dominated by churches grew up in the lands they settled. They established German-speaking schools and, despite their work ethic, found time to celebrate traditional festivals.

The newfound 'paradise' these settlers described in letters home inspired others to seek their fortune in the distant land. Johannes Stein, who had landed in the country with little or nothing in the way of worldly possessions, by dint of hard work saved enough to buy a 100-acre (40-hectare) property and run it with a staff of farmhands and servants. Another first arrival, Englebert Hahn, a carpenter from Eltville, wrote home:

> We work as human beings … we eat no black bread, our bread is made from wheat and resembles cake … what man of force and courage could hesitate between here and Germany? … I would advise you to sell everything and come.[1]

Come they did.

Between 1838 and 1839, George Angas, one of the founders of the South Australia Company, financially backed the passage of many Germans to the SA colony. They established market gardens and planted vines in what today is Australia's distinctive German district, the Barossa Valley. A second wave of migrants arrived in South Australia following their country's 1848 revolution. Mostly middle-class families, they included a large group of Catholics who settled to the north of the Barossa, in the Clare Valley, where their priests opened a college and established vineyards. In one of the largest post-revolution migrations, 300 Germans, mostly from the Rhine provinces, landed in Sydney, NSW.

Germans were among the tens of thousands from many parts of the world who streamed into the Victoria colony in the gold rush years of the 1850s. When the gold ran out many turned to farming in Victoria and NSW. By this time, the British Government, under pressure from the original white settlers in various parts of the continent, had softened its line on non-British settlers, due no doubt in part to the good reports arising from the successes of the Germans.

Post-revolution in Germany, the colony of Queensland received a steady flow of mainly Protestant Prussians, Pomeranians, Silesians and Württembergers.[2] The first arrivals were brought out in the 1840s as indentured labour to work on properties on the Darling Downs, a lush 1.6 million hectare highland of farming and grazing. Its first white settlers had been solidly British. The German labourers they brought to the area manifested the qualities of their compatriots, industrious, hard working and devout. As in the other colonies, they prospered and bought land of their own and, in turn, sponsored other Germans.

In July 1858, the *Darling Downs Gazette* reported:

A great many of our German cousins who purchased land at the recent land sales are settling in Toowoomba [the central town in the Downs district]. So great is their number that the locality where they reside [Middle Ridge] is not inaptly termed the 'German settlement'. Their buildings are erected not so much for architectural beauty as for internal comfort, but their gardens are in a high state of culture, vegetables being present [*sic*] their chief production. Some few are turning their attention to the culture of the vine, which seems to thrive tolerably well. All of them seem industrious, are temperate, and are kind, cheerful and obliging, and are on the whole a deserving class of people and we wish them every success.[3]

Among this 'deserving class' were the paternal grandparents of the major subject of this book, Walter Leslie Schwarz. His grandfather was a labourer, as was his son, Heinrich, who was born at sea in 1859 on an Australia-bound voyage. Walter's mother, Augusta Wilhelmina (Minnie) Otto, was born in 1868 (died 1942) in Ipswich, a town 70 miles (112km) by rail east of Toowoomba. She was the daughter of Andreas Wilhelm Otto and Anna Maria Elizabeth Otto (née Marquardt) who had arrived in Australia in 1864 from Uetersen in Schleswig-Holstein, Germany, formerly part of Denmark. Minnie grew up in Toowoomba. She had four children to Heinrich. Walter, the youngest, was born on 17 April 1896 when she was aged thirty.

At the time the family was living in a cottage in Herries Street, Toowoomba. Walter was given the Anglo-sounding middle name Leslie. His birth certificate shows his father anglicized his own name to 'Henry' in listing himself as the informant of the birth at the Queensland Registrar-General's Toowoomba office. On the same form, however, he gives the name 'Heinrich' as 'father of the child' and his occupation as labourer.

Henry worked at the Filch Broadfoot sawmill, where he was killed in an industrial accident before Walter was a year old. In 1897 the family moved to a less substantial cottage in an adjoining street. The owners of their new home, 11 Eleanor Street, are shown on the certificate of title as 'Augusta Wilhelmina Schwarz, widow and Walter Leslie Schwarz, minor, aged one year'.[4] The current owner, Mr David Rohde, who has researched the history of the nineteenth-century cottage, has been unable to find why a 1-year-old baby should have become part-owner of the property and ahead of his three older siblings. The family sold the house in 1923. Eleanor Street was believed to have been named after Eleanor Godsall, the wife of a Toowoomba mayor, Richard Godsall, who died in August 1885. Another Mayor Godsall, not one of Richard's five sons, officially welcomed home the rehabilitated and pardoned Schwarz at a civic reception in February 1922.

Where Schwarz received his less than adequate education is, deliberately or otherwise, confused. One source has him attending East Toowoomba State School. Another opts for Toowoomba Grammar School. Jeanette Finlayson, in her *Toowoomba & Darling Downs Family History Society Journal* article, writes he started his education at the South Toowoomba Boys' School.[5] In the Australian Dictionary of Biography, Peter Burness, author of the Schwarz entry, says he is 'believed to have been educated' at East Toowoomba public school.[6] To confuse matters, a nephew, Mr F.H. Bradley, in a letter to Burness dated 2 December 1985, said Schwarz was 'probably' educated at 'TGS' – Toowoomba Grammar School. But the grammar school records do not show him either as a pupil or among the old boys who served in the First World War. Bradley's letter was written before Burness had prepared the biography. Finlayson's details about his early life came from her own research. This confusion became an issue when Schwarz, as Merritt, was applying for a commission in the British Army to the extent that it could have exposed him.

Another Toowoomba resident of German origin, Frederick Stein, built its first town hall, described by a contemporary writer as 'handsome and commodious … with a gallery and suites of rooms for all officers of the corporation'.[7] By 1862 the corporation's public notices were being published in both English and German. The town's first Lutheran pastor arrived in 1867. By 1878 two German language newspapers emanated from Toowoomba. One, *Nord-Australische Zeitung*, circulated throughout Queensland. By the early 1890s Queensland had the highest number of German migrants of the Australian colonies. In addition to farmers and graziers, a sizeable community of merchants, tradesmen and labourers lived in and around the capital, Brisbane.

In 1863 there was an attempt to disenfranchise German residents in Toowoomba. Among those who attended a protest meeting was Alderman Flori, the town's first German-born councillor, and Henry Spiro, a Prussian Jew who became mayor in 1870. One speaker, Henry Muller, pointing out their protest had widespread public support and sympathy, went on, 'When a foreigner comes to this country, and the Government receives the naturalization fees, they are morally bound to give him the same political privilege as an Englishman or a native of the country.' He quoted Pugh's Almanac of Queensland: 'Every man twenty-one years of age who is either a natural-born or naturalized subject of Her Majesty is entitled to vote.'[8] The matter was eventually resolved in favour of the 'foreigners'. That the Germans could hold a public meeting with support from the wider community underlines how they had made a place for themselves in this prosperous part of the world while maintaining their German identity.

A decade after the attempt to remove voting rights from the non-British settlers, Pastor T. Langebecker raised another contentious issue – the teaching of the German language. At the opening of St Paul's Lutheran church school in Phillip Street, Toowoomba, Langebecker argued it was of the highest importance for children of German descent to continue to learn to speak, read and write the language. This could not be achieved by attendance at government schools. Migration from Germany would continue and in order to do business with the new migrants knowledge of their language would be indispensable. With German schools readily available, the pastor argued that parents would be foolish to throw away the opportunity for their children to be given a thorough training in German.

Contrary to the pastor's argument, by the late nineteenth century German migration had slowed to a trickle as a result of the Imperial German government's ambitions. It had earmarked surplus population for the expansion of its overseas empire.

Until the year war broke out, German National Day, 17 January, was celebrated annually in Toowoomba. Traditional festivals and celebrations were popular and German sporting and social clubs thrived. A photo, circa 1910, shows a national day parade of adults and children at Highfield or Middle Ridge, near Toowoomba, marching beneath the black, white and red Imperial German flags. By the early twentieth century an estimated 400 families of German origin were known to be in the Toowoomba region.[9]

German intelligence in pre-war years took these overt displays as showing strong levels of loyalty to the fatherland. An intelligence report compiled by Commander Zuckschwerdt of the German Navy vessel *Cormoran* in 1911, following a visit to Brisbane, claimed the state's Liberal government:

owes a great deal to the role of Queensland's Germans in the elections and thus has ample reason not to risk the support of the German element. … Moreover, because most Germans live together in settlements that bear German names, they have developed a political vitality and distinct identity that cannot be ignored by Queensland's domestic policymakers. This level of organization in the German community is supported by the numerous Protestant pastors, who in their roles as heads of parishes, are able to keep this feeling of togetherness intact and who take the lead when it comes to the pursuing of common interests.[10]

When the national census of 1911 was concluded it showed Germans were the fourth ethnic group in Australia after the English, Scots and Irish.[11] Australia's total population was 4,424,535. Of these 3,667,670 or 82.90 per cent were Australian born, while 590,722 came from the United Kingdom and 31,868 were born in New Zealand. Together they made up 96.97 per cent of the population. Australia was, as the proud boast had it, more British than the British. The German-born numbered 32,990 (0.75 per cent). However, thousands more citizens were of German origin. They were to be found in disproportionate numbers among the trades and professions, in the public service and on the benches of the state and federal parliaments. Children of German descent were attending English language–only public and private schools. As a consequence they were – our hero Schwarz among them – subject to a culture and ethos overwhelmingly British. Individuals and families had further integrated by changing their names, often for business and professional reasons. Others converted from Lutheran to what they considered to be socially acceptable denominations – Church of England, Methodist and Presbyterian. They sent sons and daughters to private schools run by these bodies.

The atmosphere of apparent acceptance and tolerance ended abruptly with the outbreak of the First World War. Pugh's words were torn up. The Federal government removed voting rights of naturalized Australians of enemy origin. Prior to the war, fifty-two schools in South Australia taught German as the main language. With the outbreak of war the SA Education Department ordered that English lessons must be taught for at least four hours a day. Under public pressure, by 1917 the state government had taken over the schools and mandated English as the sole teaching language. In Queensland the German schools simply died out, a fate Langebecker had feared was coming. Australian officials agreed with Commander Zuckschwerdt's overstated observations on the role Lutheran pastors played in the life of the German community. Wisely or otherwise, from the start of war Lutheran religious synods were banned throughout Australia. In Queensland, eight pastors were interned and after the war two were deported.[12]

Schwarz had Britain's greatest serving soldier, Field Marshal Lord Kitchener, to thank for sparking his early desire for a military career. In 1909 the newly created Commonwealth Government had invited Kitchener to Australia to advise on the setting up of a national defence force to amalgamate the individual forces of the former self-governing colonies. The following year, the field marshal presented his report, which recommended compulsory military training for all fit males over the age of twelve and a standing army of 80,000 made up of 2,000 permanents, a militia and reservists. The government accepted his advice and set the term of compulsory military service as follows: Boys aged between twelve and fourteen, known as junior cadets, were to drill for a total of 120 hours a year; cadets, aged between fourteen and eighteen, drilled for four whole days, twelve half-days and twenty-four night drills annually. From eighteen to twenty-five, men were members of the citizens' forces and required to serve sixteen whole-day drills, including eight in camp. The militia was divided into a field force and a garrison force. The former had a peacetime establishment of 16,000, to be increased to 32,000 in the event of war. The garrison peace force was 9,000, increased to 16,000. The garrison force's task was to defend vital posts in each State.[13]

Schwarz was thirteen when compulsory training began. Joining the cadet corps was a fulfilment of a 'long cherished ambition for a military career' as an officer. He says he was not in a position to apply for admission to the Royal Military College, Duntroon, due to a 'lack of means'. If he meant money, a privileged background is not a qualification for entry into an Australian military officers' training establishment. He may have been referring to his lack of educational qualifications. Given his later achievements he found a way around this barrier, with some injudicious help.

Schwarz's enthusiasm for service was not the universal reaction of the youth of the day. Between January 1912 and June 1914, 28,000 cadets were prosecuted for failing to fulfil their obligations, including 5,732 cases of boys being imprisoned.[14]

While working as a grocer's assistant Schwarz spent most of his spare time as a junior cadet to work his way through the non-commissioned ranks by studying for and passing the relevant examination, which saw him commissioned for the first time, a second lieutenant in the cadet corps. Captain Penrose, the commanding officer of Training Area 11a, took the keen young lad under his wing and within three months Schwarz had become a first lieutenant. For the next four years he imbued himself with military matters, attending classes, riding on manoeuvres with senior officers and drilling his fellow cadets, with the result that a military career became an overwhelming attraction.

At the age of eighteen came the decision that was to set in train the events that are revealed in this book: he decided to 'stop playing at soldiers' and joined the Regular Army. To do so he had to resign his prized cadet commission and enrol as a private. On 24 June 1914, he took the oath of allegiance to His Majesty for the first time and became a gunner in the Royal Garrison Artillery at Fort Lytton, Queensland, determined to work his way through the ranks to a regular commission.

War, a grim prospect to others, is for the military man the opportunity to put his training into practice, to test his character and his courage, to defend his homeland and its values. It is, in short, an ambitious young soldier's raison d'être. To Schwarz the war set the course for the life he foresaw – a future of further promotions impelled by the glory of valiant deeds and heroic battles, or a death in the noblest manner possible – on the battlefield, a soldier's death.

The life of an Australian garrison soldier had appealed to Schwarz, more so when, in the early hours of 5 August 1914, the men were roused out of their beds and told the British Empire was at war with Germany. Schwarz says that within days an enemy cargo ship had been captured. Two German steamers, *Prinz Sigismund* and the *Canstatt*, were in Queensland waters at the outbreak of war and seized as prizes by the Commonwealth Government.

Another Australian garrison made a more memorable claim in its action against an enemy ship following the declaration of war. At 7.45 am local time on 5 August (4 August in Europe) the merchant ship *Pfaltz*, no doubt having received a warning message from the German spy network operating in Australia of developments in Europe, slipped her mooring at Victoria Docks, Melbourne, and steamed into Port Phillip Bay. Before she reached the open sea the garrison at Fort Nepean fired a shot across her stern and warned that the next one would be aimed at her hull. On board, the pilot, a Mr Robinson, persuaded the captain to dock at Portsea in the bay where the ship was seized. The shot is credited with being the first fired in anger in the First World War (noon local time, when Europe was in darkness).

The young Royal Australian Garrison artillery officer who gave the order to fire was Lieutenant Morton Williams, who was to become second-in-charge of the 55th Siege Brigade's No. 2 Battery, on which Schwarz briefly served. Many years later, Williams said of the historic opening report, 'We could have shot her through the middle but we would have blown up Swan Island.' In the Second World War Williams rose to the rank of lieutenant colonel. He died in 1968 and the following year the 6-inch barrel of the gun that fired that first shot of the war was mounted at the entrance to the Portsea officer cadet school.[15]

When news reached Australia that the Germans had broken a neutrality pact by invading Belgium a patriotic fervour swept the land. Men and boys rushed to enlist. The Federal Opposition Leader, the Honorable Andrew Fisher, rashly promised, 'We shall pledge our last man and our last shilling.' More soberly, Australia's English-born prime minister, Joseph Cook offered Britain an expeditionary force of 20,000 men. Schwarz asked to be sent with this first contingent, 'either infantry or artillery'. It did not matter so long as he went. He was disappointed when told members of the Regular Forces were needed at home to train new recruits. By then Schwarz had passed his full bombardier's examination and was picked to attend classes for promotion to the rank of sergeant major.

However, behind the wave of patriotism came propaganda-fuelled anti-German discrimination. Schwarz recalls receiving a postcard, on it the words: 'When are you going to be naturalized?' Naturalized? He did not need to be. He was a British subject; his citizenship was a birthright. He writes:

> This was the first of many such insults I received, and I was continually hearing remarks, obviously directed at me about people with German names, etc, etc, should not be allowed to serve as they would probably turn traitors or some other equally disgusting remark. These remarks hurt me very much, particularly as I am very patriotic and was very keen to go on active service and do my share of the fighting.

Schwarz records that the taunts continued in the form of jokes from an instructor during the sergeant-major course. He intimates he suffered in stoic silence, possibly because he feared an outburst of anger, or a physical response, would ruin his chances of overseas service and further promotion.

Bullies quickly sense reluctance, for whatever reason, in their victims to retaliate and those who Schwarz says goaded him picked up he was not going to give vent to anger. They were, therefore, free to continue harassing and, according to Schwarz, they did. Whatever ensued, it did not affect Schwarz's promotion – at this stage. He became Temporary Sergeant Major Schwarz. Even so he claims the 'stupid persecution' did not cease.

He was detailed to Queensland's main training camp for the prime minister's expeditionary force, Enoggera, on the outskirts of the Queensland capital, Brisbane. By 3 September, more than 1,800 new recruits had moved in and the numbers grew by the day. In the following months, as the men Schwarz trained were shipped out for overseas service, rancour continued to build within him. The reason, 'I felt that I was always looked upon with suspicion.'

Ironically, in October 1914, Enoggera became an internment camp for men of German origin. Its first internees were officers and crews of the *Prinz Sigismund* and *Canstatt*. By May 1915 it had 137 detainees. In August 1915 it became an internment transit camp after the Defence Department decided to centralize internees in New South Wales, with Holsworthy by far the largest camp.

As months slipped by Schwarz began to feel he was destined to see out the war at home. He repeatedly applied to go on active service, either with his current sergeant major rank or as a private, all without success. His name was not at this stage denying him his desire for a war posting. The Minister of Defence, George Pearce, and other influential figures feared German action closer to the home front. As a result the government was reluctant to commit its best-trained troops to distant battlefields.

However, the Army found it needed to raise a siege artillery brigade for overseas service to support the infantry already abroad. To do so, promptly experienced men would have to be used – regular soldiers. It was the break Schwarz had been praying for. To join he would have to sign with the Australian Imperial Force (AIF). Its members were volunteers who had to agree to serve overseas. He did not give the condition a second thought. He promptly sent in his application. The downside was it meant demotion from his temporary sergeant major's rank. The man who had held the king's commission as a cadet officer found himself once again back in the ranks, an acting bombardier. Before he could be accepted he underwent a medical examination. His height, weight and chest measurements varied little from those found by the Royal Fusiliers doctor months later. His complexion was shown as 'fair', eyes brown and hair black. A scar was noted on the small finger of his left hand. The medical officer testified Schwarz was free of a range of diseases including scrofula, syphilis, chronic ulcers and physical deformities. He noted Schwarz could see the required distance with either eye; his heart and lungs were healthy; he had the free use of his joints and limbs; and he was not subject to fits of any description. The doctor wrote: 'I consider him fit for active service.' Those last words were music to Schwarz's ears: active service; at last it beckoned.

He and fellow volunteers from Fort Lytton took the train south to Melbourne, the Victoria state capital, where his personal details were taken down on an 'Attestation Paper of Persons Enlisted for Service Abroad, with the Australian Imperial Force'. He gave his full name, Walter Leslie Schwarz, British subject, aged 19½ years, born Toowoomba, Queensland, 24.4.1896. (His birth certificate shows 17.4.1896.) Religion, Church of England, civilian occupation, grocer.

He says 'no' to the questions had he been convicted by 'the Civil Powers' and whether he had been 'discharged from any part of His Majesty's Forces with Ignominy, or as Incorrigible and Worthless or on account of Conviction of Felony, or of a Sentence of Penal Servitude, or dismissed with Disgrace from the Navy'.

He attests: 'I Walter Leslie Schwarz do solemnly declare that the above answers made to the above questions are true, and I am willing and hereby voluntarily agree to serve in the Military Forces of the Commonwealth of Australia within or beyond the limits of the Commonwealth.' He signs *Walter Leslie Schwarz* and dates it 7-6-1915. The accompanying certificate of the Attesting Officer (signature indecipherable) shows the above questions were read to Schwarz in his presence and 'I have taken care that he understands each question and his answer to each question has been duly entered as replied to by him.' The officer ruled through the line requiring him to examine the naturalization papers of a recruit and state in his opinion they were correct. In other words, Schwarz was a bona fide British subject. These formalities complete, Schwarz swore for the second time an oath of allegiance:

> I will well and truly serve our Sovereign Lord the King in the Australian Imperial Force from 7-6-1915 until the end of the War, and a further period of four months thereafter unless sooner lawfully discharged, dismissed or removed therefrom; and that I will resist His Majesty's enemies and cause His Majesty's peace to be kept and maintained; and that I will in all matters appertaining to my service, faithfully discharge my duty according to law. So help me God.

Lieutenant Colonel Coxen, the commanding officer of the 55th Siege Artillery Brigade, certified Schwarz's attestation as correct and that he had complied with the required forms. 'I accordingly approve and appoint him,' Coxen wrote over his signature. Schwarz was given pay book number 256 and the rank of gunner.

Schwarz swore the oath to go on active service for reasons both abstract and practical, an escape from persecution, a chance to truly serve his king in battle and to further his career.

Chapter 2

'Plans Already Made'

The 55th Artillery Brigade embarked on board HMAT (His Majesty's Australian Transport ship) *Orsova*, the passenger liner built in 1909 and converted into a troop carrier, which sailed from Port Melbourne on 17 July 1915, with Schwarz hoping the serious business of what they were about would bring an end to the harassment. He insists it did not. However, he continued his resolve not to lose his temper or respond aggressively. During the voyage he saw the consequences of an ill-tempered argument. Gunner Alf Campbell threw a blow that connected with Sergeant Morley's face. In the subsequent on board court martial Campbell claimed he had lost his temper because Morley had reported him for using improper language to another non-commissioned officer (NCO). The court sentenced Campbell to sixty days' gaol, to be followed by discharge 'with ignominy from His Majesty's Services'.[1] Given his mindset such a fate would have been harder for Schwarz to endure than anything he'd been putting up with since the war began.

The brigade settled into camp in south-east England, near the ancient Kent village of Lydd, and resumed training. (Schwarz says that the brigade arrived in Lydd 'about June 1915'. This is one of a number of problems he has with dates. In this case, the 17 July date quoted at the outset of this chapter as the brigade's departure date is taken from official records. As we have seen, he had enlisted in the AIF in Melbourne in June, signing on and swearing allegiance to the king on 7 June 1915.) It was here, we learn, that the matter of Schwarz's antecedents took a more serious turn. He writes it began with rumours that men of German origin were to be kept away from the fighting. At first, Schwarz put such talk down to the men who had been relentlessly targeting him. How could he be overlooked? He was a professional; he was better trained than half the brigade and his presence on the battlefront would be invaluable. He tells us that during this time he had been selected for a three-week course for battery commanders' assistants, in which he gained 'the highest number of marks' of all participants. Following the course he was assigned for duty with Major Hurst's Number Two battery crew and, Schwarz says, the major found him to be a first-rate assistant.

The brigade's training was due to culminate in a series of field days attended by the top British brass. Schwarz had been looking forward to them. As with any soldier worth his salt, he wanted to put what he had learnt and trained for into practice in both the field exercises and the real thing – active service. However, without warning or explanation, and to his surprise, 'I was taken off the battery commander's staff' – he does not say whether by direct or written order – and given a lowly job, mess orderly. This was a non-combatant's role. Schwarz had to have been more than surprised, devastated.

With the military career in which he had invested years of work and study hanging in the balance, Schwarz says he decided to give the 55th Brigade's officers a final chance to deny the rumours that men such as he would not be crossing to France. On the morning of 23 October he approached Lieutenant Colonel Walter Coxen, the brigade's commanding officer. Coxen, then aged forty-four, was, like Schwarz, a career soldier. He was to rise to the rank of brigadier general by war's end. Described by the commander of the Australian Corps as 'one of the most able of our Australian artillery officers', Sir John Monash went on to say command of the Artillery Corps might be 'just a little too big for him. He is a dour, sour, unsympathetic creature and difficult to get on with.'[2]

From what we are able to read into Schwarz's experience, Monash's view of the colonel's lack of sympathy was confirmed. Coxen listened in silence as Schwarz pointed out he'd done his duty under Major Hurst, who had given him good reports. He had fully expected to be a member of the major's crew for the field days. Schwarz goes on to say that in response to his plea Coxen suggested he take the matter up with 'my battery commander', that is, Hurst. Until Schwarz was removed from Hurst's crew it had been his understanding that the two of them would go to war together as part of a team, that they both were like-minded in their approach to tasks and their mutual appreciation of the need for discipline and constant training. Schwarz had been under the impression in their months together a mutual respect had grown between them. As Schwarz puts it, at this final interview between the two it appeared Hurst did not share Schwarz's view of their relationship. The officer gave 'evasive answers to my direct questions as to whether my German name had anything to do with it,' Schwarz writes. 'He therefore decided that his suppositions were correct and that my services were not required with ... the brigade ...' That being the case he would put 'plans already made into execution'.

Later that morning – Saturday, 23 October 1915 – Gunner Schwarz walked out of the Australian Imperial Forces 55th Battery Siege Brigade, never to return. At Lydd Station he boarded a train and an hour later arrived in London, where he was to spend the rest of the weekend. By leaving the base without permission he had declared himself AWL (absent without leave). He had not applied for a leave pass and does not appear to have worried that he would be stopped and arrested by the military police.

Swinging London

War had brought a marked change to London, shaking loose the final pillars of the Victorian era. The capital of the British Empire had become in many ways what a later generation was to brand 'swinging'. Most obvious was the behaviour of women, particularly young women. The war had given them an independence an older generation could not have imagined. Their new morality was reflected in their attitudes and freedom of movement. Prior to 1914, young women would not have been seen walking alone in London streets, not if they valued their reputation. Now they asserted their right to come and go as they pleased at all hours. They had taken to wearing make-up in public, adopted the brassiere in place of the camisole and their skirts had begun to rise from the first months of war to reveal first the ankle, then the mid-calf. Many women had moved to the capital from the provinces to take up war work and with it came good money, independence from family and local constraints and a desire to make the most of their new freedom while the opportunity lasted.

Young women took up smoking, drinking and drugs. They hung out alone or in groups in pubs, restaurants, nightclubs and dance halls. They swung to the beat of American ragtime and jazz.

Pubs were open from early morning until late at night to cater for shift workers, soldiers on leave and others citizens caught up the atmosphere of eat, drink and be merry, for who knows what tomorrow may bring. Hundreds of nightclubs had blossomed in the Soho area. Naturally enough in such a charged atmosphere, sex was an inevitable ingredient of the pleasures to be had. A woman historian of the time, M.A. Hamilton, commented: 'Life was less than cheap; it was thrown away … Little wonder that the old ideals of chastity and self control in sex were, for many, also lost.'[3]

As a result of the Gallipoli campaign, the honeymoon period for members of the Australian and New Zealand Army Corps (Anzacs) in London was at its peak by October 1915. Press and pulpit praised and feted the Diggers and Kiwis. Members of the upper classes invited them to stay at their stately homes. Hotels, shops and the growing number of prostitutes wooed the men from Down Under. The fact that the Australian private was paid five shillings a day, in contrast to the bob-a-day British Tommy, added to their attraction. An AIF corporal's daily pay was nine shillings, whilst at the other end of the ranks a lieutenant colonel earned £1 17s 6d and a colonel or brigadier £2 5s 0d a day. The Anzacs' money flowed into theatres, both live and cinema, musical revues with semi-naked chorus girls and Charlie Chaplin comedies. For those of a more serious mien, Shakespearian plays continued at the Old Vic throughout the war. In 1915, the adult pantomime *Chu Chin Chow* was well into its record run of 2,000 performances. On the weekend of Schwarz's final visit to the capital as an Australian soldier, a new Anglo-French revue, *Honi Soit*, had opened at the London Pavilion. It was billed as offering merry and bright entertainment.

The Times that Saturday carried news that showed the authorities had decided the good times were sapping the war effort and must be curbed. Opening hours of pubs in London were to be restricted from November to between noon and 2.30 pm and 6.00 pm to 9.00 pm for the foreseeable future. (They remained restricted with minor variations until late in the twentieth century.) Although nightclubs were at the same time ordered closed by 10.30 pm, the effect was to drive the late-nighters underground. As soon as law enforcers closed one down another took its place.[4] David Lloyd George, who became British Prime Minister the following year, intoned, 'We are fighting Germans, Austrians and Drink and so far as I can see the greatest of these deadly foes is Drink.'[5]

The openness and moral freedom of women was a tempting lure for young men fresh from the bloody battlefield of the Dardanelles and raw recruits from the provinces and empire. Many had grown up in empire towns such as Schwarz's Toowoomba, where women did not smoke, drink or openly flirt, certainly not in public places. There is no suggestion that Schwarz was tempted or that he either approved or disapproved of the behaviour of the London lasses. We do know he did not contract venereal disease. The VD rate among Australians in England at 144 per thousand was higher than that of the British Army, 34 per thousand.[6] Not all liaisons between Australian soldiers and English women were based on a 'good time' or paid sex. By December 1918, the rate of marriage between Australian soldiers and British woman had reached 150 a week. By war's end, the number of 'war brides' was 5,626. In all, 15,386 wives, children, fiancées and dependents returned to Australia with the AIF in 1919.[7]

More than a thousand officers and men on the staff of the Australian Imperial Force were permanently based in the capital. The AIF HQ building was a Wesleyan theological college in Horseferry Road, taken over for the duration. It was around the corner from the Australian High Commission at that time in Victoria Street, Westminster. HQ was a busy place. Reinforcements from Australia were received there and soldiers on leave could leave their kit at its quartermaster's store for safekeeping while others picked up new clothes. Clerks organized rail passes, and soldiers cashed their pay slips and posted letters home.

English hospitals by October 1915 were treating more than 7,000 Australian and 4,000 New Zealand casualties. Many were in the 3rd London General Hospital, Wandsworth, and the County of London War Hospital at Woodcote Park, near Epsom Downs. From these hospitals convalescents either recovered and returned to the fighting or were shipped back to Australia, their fighting days over. Those recovering who could get about were out in force on 'swinging' London's streets as usual that late October weekend, doing their best to enjoy the hospitality the city had to offer, although their financial means of doing so were nowhere near those of Schwarz's and others who had yet to taste battle. In October the New South Wales Agent General, a Mr R.R. Wise, had complained to the Australian High Commissioner, Sir George Reid, the wounded men were penniless as they were not paid while in hospital. Furthermore, 'the men suffer from cold and this is regrettable in view of the large supplies of warm clothing sent from NSW. Complaints are all due to want of organization. The War Contingent Committee is ineffective to deal with them.'[8] Australians and New Zealanders living in London had set up a committee with premises near AIF headquarters originally to provide boarding establishments and a buffet that served free meals.

HQ was also the home of the Australian Provost Corps, that is, military police (MPs). They had a reputation for toughness. Soldiers who fell into their hands found it an unpleasant experience. The MPs patrolled the streets and those places where soldiers ate, drank, rested and sought diversion from the realities of war. One place on their list was the Union Jack Club in Sandell Street, opposite Waterloo Station. It provided low-priced and comfortable accommodation for British and empire soldiers in both world wars.

When Schwarz left Charing Cross Station he walked along the Strand and over Waterloo Bridge to the club where he booked a bed. Based on facts uncovered during my research it may be assumed Schwarz's booking was in military terms a feint, a manoeuvre to hide the fact he had a prearranged safe house in which to shelter.

It was not all whisky and wild women for the Diggers. They also 'did' the sights – the Houses of Parliament, Big Ben, Westminster Abbey – those places they had learnt as schoolboys to regard as proud monuments to the empire. 'The letters and postcards they sent home were redolent of the excited and slightly naive "tourist" attitude of many of the men.'[9] Some London landmarks, including Buckingham Palace, had steel nets draped over their roofs, the object being to deflect bombs dropped by Zeppelins, the giant dirigibles that had begun appearing over London at night since February 1915. The buildings their bombs destroyed or damaged provided new sites for 'tourists'.

The Diggers' English honeymoon had begun to fade by 1916. After the first favourable impressions of England had worn off, Diggers' letters and postcards home lost their touristy touch; London was no longer the shining capital of a great empire, but a city of slums, gritty buildings and grubby people. Diggers complained among themselves of conditions both in their camps and hospitals; the English climate was woeful, the people snobs while the shopkeepers, girls of the nights, in fact, anyone with whom they dealt, was liable to rip them off. On the other side of the fading relationship the British press had begun to write of the Anzacs as over-praised. Rowdiness, drunkenness and an increasing number of Diggers appearing before magistrates on various misdemeanours and crimes added to the disillusion of the Bronzed Anzacs. By 1918, their reputation as 'womanizers' had the British War Cabinet considering whether the Australians should be kept from London altogether and repatriated as soon as possible. Schwarz was by then a decorated British officer, the city welcoming him as a hero from one of its own regiments.

Schwarz says he spent the weekend acquiring civilian clothes without saying from where. He gives a clue in a letter to his mother written prior to his desertion – a place where few questions would be asked.

> You have heard of Petticoat Lane I suppose. Well I was down there last Sunday morning; by Jove, it is a funny place, all sorts & kinds of men selling different things from a needle to an anchor [sic].[10]

It is most likely that with what clothes he bought, or had bought for him either here or elsewhere, he ended up looking much like other recruits of the body he was about to join, the Sportsman's Battalion. Its potential members arrived at its recruiting depot in mostly casual clothes, old school scarves, rugby jerseys, cricket club caps and jumpers. Some fronted in riding and hunting outfits based on the assumption they were joining a mounted outfit and among them were those who had offered to bring their own horses. For Schwarz similar clothes would have sufficed as adequate for his new persona as the Australian-born son of an Englishman.

However, if we were to accept that Schwarz's enlistment was above board then it was not only in his appearance he had to be convincing. A slip of the tongue, a careless word, or a long a pause in responding to questions and his life would unravel, his war would be over. He would face not the Soldier's Death he believed to be the noblest of all deaths, but a soldier's disgrace, and that would break his mother's heart.

An aside: a glance at the roster of Sportsman's Battalion members shows as solid a list of British surnames as would have been found on the roll of a public school's roster of the time ... Maitland, Bull, Gardner, Lewis, Spencer, Albany, Bryden, Goodfellow, Harvey, Jones, Madgwick, Parsons and so on. It conjures a thought: had Schwarz's true name appeared on that roster it would be as startling a sight as a photo of Tommies with a man in a German uniform in their midst.

Chapter 3

'Play up Play up and Play THE Game'

In Britain, with the outbreak of war, local authorities, industrialists and committees of private citizens raised army units independently of the War Office. They were known as Pals battalions. They comprised men from a particular city or district, or from common social and occupational backgrounds, such as the great public schools. In many case it was the social cohesion of the British class system that bound the members of these units. I discuss later whether Schwarz was guided in his selection or acted on his own initiative when he approached the Sportsman's, which was one of the Pals units. Its common interest was, of course, sport in all its variations. At its inception there was a further matter the members shared in common: sport at a competent level in this era was the province of the leisured classes.

By 1915, the original ethos for the battalion had slipped somewhat but not entirely. Therefore, why did a man on the run from authorities, from a working class background, choose to enlist in this high profile unit into which problems of assimilation could be his undoing? Suffice to say at this stage the unit had an added attraction that may have countered any fears of rejection or exposure: A disproportionate number of officers were being commissioned from the Sportsman's ranks, on the assumption its members were innately qualified to lead. Schwarz had believed since his cadet days he was a leader.

The first Sportsman's Battalion was raised at a meeting chaired by Mrs E. Cunliffe-Owen at the Hotel Cecil in the Strand, London, on 25 September 1914. She had first sought permission from Field Marshal Earl Kitchener, at that time Secretary of State for War. She and her husband, Edward, were cousins. The two were related to the Royal Family and had other influential political and social connections. She was the daughter of Sir Philip Cunliffe-Owen. Her brother, Sir Hugo, worked for the Ministry of Information during the First World War and for this he was created a baronet. Hugo became a director of the British-American Tobacco Company on its formation in 1902, and was its chairman from 1923 until his retirement in 1945. For the last two years of his life he was president of the company. Edward was educated at Wellington and Trinity College, Cambridge. He was a barrister, the only son of Colonel Henry Cunliffe-Owen of the Royal Engineers. The couple had two daughters and a son, who was the godson of Queen Alexandra. Aged seventeen, the boy was commissioned in the 2nd Sportsman's Battalion, where he was its youngest recruit.[1]

Mrs Cunliffe-Owen not only had Kitchener's blessing to form the battalions, but using her influence obtained a concession from him to allow men aged up to forty-five years of age to join. Until then men of this age had been barred from war service.[2] It is a mystery to this day why Mrs Owen wanted older men in a battalion when its emphasis was on fit young men in the prime of life, of fine physique, 'inured to outdoor life, good shots, and all keen sportsmen'.[3] By 1916, battalion commander Lieutenant Colonel H. Vernon sent all men aged more than forty back to base camp.[4]

Among the original members were college rowing crews, big-game hunters, mountaineers and cricketers. The latter included two current members of the England team, Patsy Hendren and Andrew Sandham. Also enlisted were thirty-nine of the country's best rugby players including ex-public schoolboys who had played for England. Its posters emphasized team spirit: 'Join together, train together, embark together, fight together.' A final unction, 'die together', must be implied. The posters also carried, the line familiar to schoolboys throughout the British Empire: 'Play up Play up and Play THE [sic] Game', from Sir Henry Newbolt's *Vitaï Lampada* (see Appendix 3).

Mrs Cunliffe-Owen took an active part in the formation of the battalion. This included personal letters appealing for donations. Another source of income was the three guineas joining fee each recruit was charged. As we have seen, the British private was paid a shilling a day so the joining fee acted as a deterrent for those of lesser means. Schwarz was not apparently deterred by the fee. In addition to private income, the War Office provided £20,000 towards the cost of establishing and supplying the battalion.[5]

Most London recruits for Regular units enlisted at their local drill hall. However, would-be Sportsmen initially had to present themselves to its recruiting office at the Hotel Cecil. Completed in 1896, the Cecil stood between the Thames Embankment and the Strand. Named after the Cecil family, who had occupied a home on the site from the seventeenth century, it was by the start of the First World War a fashionable venue for London society. As well as being the place where the Sportsman's Battalion was founded, it was also the wartime headquarters of the newly formed Royal Air Force (RAF). The hotel, with its 800 rooms, was largely demolished in 1930, and Shell Mex House was built on the site. The Strand facade of the hotel remains, occupied by shops and offices, with, at its centre, a grandiose arch leading to Shell Mex House proper. In March 2008 a plaque commemorating the RAF's formation was affixed to the building. There is nothing to show that this was also the place where so many fit and healthy young men swapped their pleasurable lives for the grim reality of war, among them those who made the supreme sacrifice.

Mrs Cunliffe-Owen took over the hotel's India Room for recruiting purpose. Here a Royal Fusiliers officer sat at a green baize-covered table with a large ledger recording the names and other details of potential candidates.

When members of its 1st Battalion moved into barracks at Grey Towers, Hornchurch, Essex, in October 1915, Mrs Cunliffe-Owen held a lavish reception with many a celebrity as guests. Queen Alexandria sent an autographed sketch of herself as well as one of King Edward. These were hung in the officers' mess, along with portraits of the then King George V and Queen Mary.[6] George was Colonel-in-Chief of the battalion.

It appears the lavish event marked the height of Mrs Cunliffe-Owen's involvement with the Sportsman's. Months before, she had appeared in court and been fined £5 in a case involving an overdue payment to a local butcher. This was not the only financial problem that may have distracted her from patriotic activity. Private W.S. Ferrie, a Glasgow University graduate, who joined the 2nd Battalion, heard she was involved in a bankruptcy case. Ferrie hinted that the three-guinea joining fee recruits were asked to pay was somehow suspiciously involved.[7]

By 1915 the British Army had absorbed the 1st Sportsman's as the 23rd Royal Fusiliers attached to the 86th Brigade. The word 'fusilier' originated as a name for troops armed with flintlock muskets known as 'fusils'. The first fusiliers comprised ten companies that Sir Walter Vane raised to fight the French in Holland in 1674. Since then fusiliers units have been part of British military history. The Royal Regiment of Fusiliers grew out of amalgamations of these individual units.

From the time the cry of battle first sounded men have lied and cheated to join the colours. Their reasons have often been less than noble: to escape domestic responsibilities and/or bad debts, to hide criminal records and so on. Conversely, the generals and their minions have turned a blind eye to such foibles in their need to fill ranks reduced by death, injury and the reluctance of others less keen to march away to war. An example and a coincidence: on the day Schwarz became a deserter, 23 October 1915, AIF Private Albert Neil (real name Hugo Ludolff) was court martialled, charged with breaking out of Langwarrin Military Camp, in Victoria, Australia. Ludolff told the court that although he'd been born in Sydney, his father was German. Unlike Schwarz he'd changed his name before enlisting 'on account of certain troubles', which he was not asked to specify. Nor was he asked how long before enlisting had he adopted his alias. Ludolff, who had previous convictions for going AWL, was sentenced to ninety days jail and subsequent discharge – the sentence was suspended subject to his good behaviour.[8] His records do not show anything to indicate that the disclosure of his real name subsequently led to the kind of discrimination of which Schwarz complained. The point to be made here is that a desire to commit noble deeds in battle is rarely found in men who join the Army using an alias and lying about their past. Schwarz's case was also rare in that he swore twice under his real name and once using his alias to truly serve the king.

Before deserting, we must assume Schwarz, or someone posing as him, presented himself to the Hotel Cecil under the name Walter Lancelot Merritt. Had it been Schwarz (out of AIF uniform) he would have impressed physically. Recruits needed to be a minimum of 5 feet 6 inches in height, with a chest measurement of 35½ inches. Schwarz was 5 feet 11 inches tall and his chest measured 37 inches. Whether it was Schwarz or a stand-in, the officer at the desk gave him a pass mark after an oral examination and handed him a form to take to a medical examination.

On 25 October 1915, a cool, overcast day, as it had been for most of the weekend, Schwarz presented himself along with other potential recruits to the Royal Fusiliers depot in Scotland Yard, Whitehall. On the form from the Cecil was written his alias, Walter Lancelot Merritt. The young man was imbued, as we have seen, with the qualities inherited by his settler forebears: hard working, religious, honest and upright. These were qualities he lived by before and after the war. They were not the qualities he took with him to the recruiting depot. Along with the truth, moral principles are among the early casualties of war.

In the forms he filled in he stated he was the 21-year-old son of Henry Merritt, an Englishman who had migrated to Australia. His place of birth was Parish Melbourne, County Australia; religion, C of E (Church of England – Anglican); and his next of kin, Nellie Merritt of James Street, Toowoomba, Queensland.[9]

While undergoing his induction examination, King George was making a public appeal for more recruits. The end, the reigning monarch told his subjects, 'is not in sight'. *The Evening News*, London, on the same day reported a pronounced increase of applications by 'eligibles' (men of military age) for passports to leave Britain. In Australia that weekend *The Sydney Morning Herald* had published the latest Anzac casualty list from the Dardanelles campaign: 297 officers and 4,976, men killed or wounded, to bring the total up to 27,400. It reported British casualties for Flanders between 26 September and 13 October 1915 as 2,068 officers and 30,886 men killed or wounded.

On the face of it, volunteers were scarce. Nevertheless, it had not reached the stage where any man could walk into a recruiting depot and be accepted without question. A recruit needed to fill in forms, answer questions, undergo a physical examination and take a solemn oath. Officers were duty-bound to warn potential recruits of the severe penalties should they lie or make false attestations.

The battalion medical officer (a retired fleet surgeon whose signature is illegible on Schwarz's papers) noted four vaccination marks on

Schwarz's left arm. These were for smallpox and enteric fever. The doctor did not fill in the 'when vaccinated' details; travellers between England and Australia at the time were vaccinated as a matter of course. In all likelihood the doctor did not bother with this detail, more concerned with moving the recruit along for any number of reasons, including the fact that others were waiting in line. He missed the scar on the small finger of Schwarz's right hand. Despite these lapses, the doctor satisfied himself as to Schwarz's state of health, marking it down as excellent. The officer noted the fact he was taller than the average Tommy, with a wider chest expansion – a perfect psychical fit for the Sportsman's.

The MO passed him back to the duty approving officer, a Captain Rickard, who produced Army Form B2505, a standard Short Service form for men enlisting for the duration of the war. Rickard cautioned the Australian that if he falsely answered any of the questions about to be put to him he would be liable to be punished as provided by the Army Act. He then called in a witness (identified as a J. Jordan of the Royal Fusiliers), produced pen and ink and told Schwarz to fill out the form in Jordan's presence. Schwarz did so as follows:

Q.1	What is your name?	Walter Lancelot Merritt.
Q.2	What is your full address?	23 Warrender Road, Holborn.
Q.3	Are you a British subject?	Yes.
Q.4	What is your age?	21.
Q.5	What is your trade or calling?	Clerk.
Q.6	Are you married?	No.
Q.7	Have you ever served in any branch of His Majesty's Forces, naval or military, if so state particulars?	No.
Q.7a	Have you truly stated the whole, if any, of your previous service.	Yes.
Q.8	Are you willing to be vaccinated or re-vaccinated?	Yes.
Q.9	Are you willing to be enlisted for General Service?	Yes.

Q.10   Did you receive a Notice and do you   Yes. J. Henderson,
   understand its meaning, and who   R.Fus.
   gave it to you?

Q. 11   Are you willing to serve for the   Yes.
   duration of the war provided His
   Majesty should so long require
   your services?

Schwarz then swore the 'above answers made by me to the above questions are true and I am willing to fulfil the engagements made'. He signed, Walter Lancelot Merritt and Jordan signed as having witnessed Schwarz's responses and signature. Merritt took the oath:

> I swear by Almighty God that I will be faithful and bear true allegiance to His Majesty King George the Fifth, His Heirs and Successors and that I will, as in duty-bound, honestly and faithfully defend His Majesty, His Heirs and Successors, in Person, Crown and dignity against all enemies, and will observe and obey all orders of His Majesty, His Heirs and Successors, and of the Generals and Officers set over me. So help me God.

Schwarz and the other freshly sworn recruits were sent to the Fusilier's depot at Gidea Park, Romford, where he was put on the roll of the 30th (Royal Fusiliers) reserve battalion. There is possibility Schwarz may have originally been a member of the Congregational church. The Church of England unequivocally supported the war.[10] Its predominant position in 1915 was summed up by the Bishop of London, who called on the nation to mobilize for a Holy War. 'Christ died ... for freedom, honour and chivalry and our boys are dying for the same thing,' said Bishop Winnington-Ingram.[11] In choosing the knightly name 'Lancelot', Schwarz may have been moved to consider matters honourable and chivalrous by the hymn 'The Supreme Sacrifice', sung during the war in English public schools and at memorial and dedication services for those old boys who had died in action:

O valiant hearts, who to your glory came,
Through dust of conflict and through battle-flame;
Tranquil you lie, your knightly virtue proved,
Your memory hallowed in the Land you loved.[12]

Together with the bishop's exhortation, the words comforted and inspired young men, among them those who were to make the supreme sacrifice while bishops slept sound in their beds.

A new life began for Schwarz within the ranks of the Sportsman's 30th (Reserve) Battalion. No. 4233 Private Walter Lancelot Merritt, a supposed raw recruit, had first to be kitted out. Because of his psychical stature – not unusual for the Sportsman's – he was given the largest size the British Army had in greatcoat, tunic and trousers. The sleeves and legs still needed lengthening. Recruits were given two kit bags, in which they stowed a haversack (which held knife, fork and spoon, button stick, cardigan, razor, brass brushes for shaving and polishing), two pairs of strong boots, two pairs of puttees, two pairs of underpants, two sets of gold regimental numbers to be worn on shoulder flaps, two towels, three bluish-grey shirts, three pairs of socks and a groundsheet. For many new recruits in the British Army, though not necessarily in the 1st Sportsman's, the equipment represented the largest wardrobe they'd possessed to that stage of their lives. The new equipment that would take it was stamped by signwriters in black ink with the regiment's name and the soldier's number.

The store clerks also gave Schwarz and his fellow recruits a large brown paper sheet in which to wrap their civilian clothes and other personal non-army issue items. Tied with string the parcels were stored away – after the recruit had written his home address on them. The parcels were kept for recovery at the end of the war or were posted to a relative upon the death of the owner. Schwarz had been through similar kitting-out processes three times before, as a cadet, on joining the Regular Army and with the AIF. Therefore he would have known of a procedure for the disposal of his civilian belongings. In the past he'd had a valid address, his mother's home in Toowoomba. He does not say what address he scribbled on his package when he joined the Fusiliers.

There were thirty men to a hut, their beds consisting of three planks laid on two trestles. A straw mattress and four blankets covered the planks.

In the following months, as a new recruit with allegedly no previous service, Schwarz would have had to sit through lectures and undertake basic training he must have known by heart covering military procedures, care of his uniform, personal hygiene, the meaning of the various stripes, pips and badges on uniforms, who to address as 'sir' and so on. They would have been no more than minor irritants compared to the greater feeling that he was at last free of abuse, innuendo and suspicion. He was one of them; an Englishman. With this enormous weight off his shoulders and his fears of exposure fading by the day, he obviously revelled in the real training, the prospects of promotion and the promise that it was only a matter of time before he was in the battle.

Schwarz, not a modest young man when it came to his army career, wrote: 'I found myself a paid lance corporal within a very few days.' Actually, it was weeks. A month later he had been promoted again, to full corporal. Schwarz credits his promotions with the fact that he quickly settled down to the new conditions in which he found himself and the knowledge he displayed, which enabled him to come out top of a course of physical drill and bayonet fighting, although such a course is not shown on his service record. He'd had to climb out of the lower ranks before this. His training as a cadet had stood him in good stead for promotion in the Regular Army. He had reached the rank of sergeant major before circumstances had him demoted. He was as determined as ever to try again. Joining the Fusiliers had been the first step in the process and it was paying off.

Chapter 4

'Extremely Top Secret'

From early in the war the attitude in Australia towards its German community had followed the Home Country's lead. One of the first wartime measures the Australian Government introduced, the War Precautions Act, authorized local military commandants to intern 'enemy subjects with whose conduct they were not satisfied'. It also gave the Minister for Defence, George Pearce (who years later was involved in the granting of the pardon of Schwarz), the power to order the detention of naturalized subjects should he form the opinion they were 'disaffected or disloyal'.[1] The Act, passed by Parliament on 29 October 1914, was later extended to cover natural-born British subjects of enemy descent.

A further Act, the Trading with the Enemy Act, imposed heavy fines and imprisonment for those who attempted to make profits through companies that had commercial connections with German or Austrian businesses. For some, profit proved more persuasive than patriotism and there were constant breaches. By June 1917, forty-four firms had been prosecuted.[2] Other measures included the banning of German language newspapers and, in one of the worst small-minded examples of discrimination, the South Australian conservative coalition government deleted sixty-nine German place names from the maps of the state and replaced them with English or Aboriginal names. In Queensland the Toowoomba council changed the name of one of its main streets, named in honour of Frederick Stein, who built the first town hall, to Jellicoe, after the British admiral. In the post-war years, many original names were restored, but 'Jellicoe' Street remains to this day.

As for propaganda, in May 1915 the British Government released a report that alleged German soldiers had committed atrocities in occupied Belgium. A committee, headed by Lord Bryce, whose background gave it more credibility than it subsequently warranted, compiled the report. Bryce had been Professor of Civil Law at Oxford University and had received honorary degrees from several German universities prior to the war. He had served as a Liberal member of parliament and been British ambassador to Washington between 1907 and 1913.

More than 1,000 Belgian refugees who had fled to Britain testified before the committee that the invading Germans had committed rape, torture and murder on a large scale. The refugees' stories were what the committee members wanted to hear – truth being, as Schwarz' story shows, in short supply in war.

The committee report had the effect on the public in Britain and Australia as defined by psychological warfare expert Charles Roetter:

> It made the enemy appear degraded, foul and incapable of humane or decent instincts; if humankind were to be saved these people had to be destroyed.[3]

In Britain, the upshot of its release was a wave of anti-German riots across the country. On 12 May 1915 London's *Evening News* reported marauding mobs in London's East End and Smithfield Market areas:

> Hundreds of men and women took part in a disgraceful orgy of shop smashing and looting. The mob did not discriminate between naturalized and non-naturalized Germans and some of those whose premises were shattered have carried on business without molestation for ten or twenty years. Upwards of 80 per cent [of Smithfield meat market firms] are now exhibiting the notice 'No business transacted with Germans'.

The Bryce report first appeared in *The Times*, giving it the stamp of establishment authority and authenticity. Historians cited its republishing in Australian newspapers as bringing to the boil feelings already stirred by earlier published stories of German atrocities and other unscrupulous behaviour. Newspapers had found that such reports, whether or not they were verified, were circulation boosters.[4] One widely published claim was that the Germans had crucified a Canadian soldier by pinning him with bayonets to the wooden fence of a farm building. English poet and novelist Robert Graves, who did not believe the story, credited its circulation with causing the Canadians to share with the Australians the worst reputation for violence against German prisoners.[5]

Despite her English ancestry, the mother of a South Australian hero, Lieutenant Edward Mattner, was publicly insulted at a conscription referendum polling booth. Her husband's forebears were German migrants.

Lutheran Pastor Peter Faggotter of Toowoomba told me a retired pastor recalled arsonists burnt churches on the Darling Downs, although the pastor was not confident in identifying which churches. Lyall Kupke, the national Lutheran Church Archivist, said, to his knowledge, arsonists attacked three of the denomination's churches during the war. The first was Netherby Lutheran Church, torched on 7 May 1915. Netherby is north-east of Nhill in Victoria. St Luke's Lutheran Church, Murtoa, also in Victoria, was burnt down on 6 April 1916 and St John's, in Edithburgh, South Australia, was destroyed on 5 October 1918. Kupke said arsonists destroyed at least two others after the war – Forster in SA in 1920 and Bendigo, Victoria, in 1925.

On Saturday, 15 January 1916, under the heading 'ANTI-GERMAN RIOTS, FORTY PERSONS ARRESTED', *The Sydney Morning Herald* published one of the few accounts of a mob attack to be recorded in Australian newspapers. The report reflects the earlier *Evening News* account with the exception that police arrested many of those involved in the Australia riot.

The report:

Melbourne, Friday: Chapel-street, Prahran, for the past two days has been the scene of an attack of Germanphobia, which on Thursday evening reached something close to a riot, the windows of the shop of Geo. Ikinger being broken. Another pastry cook's shop occupied by Johann Plisch, Greville Street, close to the railway station, also had its windows smashed for which offense five soldiers were arrested this morning. The man in charge of Ikinger's cart was mobbed and pelted with tarts and other pastry. Shops of a number of persons in Chapel-street bearing German names were attacked this evening by soldiers and a crowd singing 'Australia will be there'.

Persuasion by the police only led to insults and Constable Montieth received a blow to the head from behind necessitating surgical treatment.

Chapel-street, as is usual on Friday night, was densely crowded and thousands rolled up near the Town Hall where Ikinger's shop is situated. Military and civil police strove to maintain order, but even ordinarily quiet women became termagants and tried to bite and kick the police. At every arrest the crowd hooted and yelled and before peace was restored forty persons were arrested, chiefly for insulting behaviour. The riots lasted for several hours, quiet not being restored until past 11 o'clock.

In Australia, as this report shows, police did not look the other way when individuals were set upon or German-owned properties attacked. Where there was discrimination in society the driving force may have had as much to do with anti-German sentiment as with the exercise of human traits of jealousy, greed, revenge or opportunism, in the form of long-suppressed grievances erupting among neighbours, business and professional competitors and others. Historian Sir Ernest Scott (1867–1939) cites cases involving workers demanding their bosses sack fellow workers who were of German nationality or heritage, professionals of German background who were dismissed from universities and the public service, neighbours who denounced neighbours, businessmen who refused to deal with others who had German names no matter how long they had done so pre-war.[6] The Attorney General of South Australia, the Honorable H. Homburg, who was born in the SA capital Adelaide, quit his portfolio and the seat he had held since 1906 claiming he had been forced to do so because of his heritage.

A further measure passed in April 1917, the Commonwealth Electoral (War-Time) Act deprived naturalized Germans and others born in enemy countries of the right to vote.[7] This angered one serving soldier enough to pen a letter to the 'British-Australasian' magazine protesting it was an outrageous injustice to his loyal relatives. Under the nom de plume 'Private', he used a sentence similar to the one Schwarz used in his petition to describe his feelings – 'These remarks hurt me very much.' Private wrote:

this has hurt me very much. She [his mother] has two sons fighting for the empire, one in France (myself) and one in Palestine. Her brother also was refused a vote; he had two sons also fighting, one killed in action on the Somme last year and the other serving in the -th [*sic*] Battalion ... Mother was bred and born in Australia and a more loyal woman never lived. She worked hard in every respect toward assisting the troops on this side, she paid particular attention to the Red Cross, and now all her work has gone by refusing her a vote. I am really hurt that much that I can hardly explain the position to you, to think that me and my brother are away fighting for our country and she treated like that.[8]

The letter may also be taken as evidence that not all men of German origin serving in the AIF were suffering the discrimination claimed by Schwarz; it appears any hurt they were experiencing came from treatment meted out to their relatives at home rather than from fellow soldiers.

Most civilians arrested under the War Precautions Act were interned in Holsworthy camp on the outskirts of Sydney. One politician took a pragmatic and sensible stand when confronted with a demand that all Germans and persons of German origin be interned. The New South Wales Attorney General, the Honorable D.R. Hall, pointed out the number of German-born residents in Australia was more than 30,000 while thousands more were of German origin:

They are engaged in growing wheat, building houses, boot making and a variety of other occupations ... That means ... Australians will grow wheat for them, build houses for them, make boots for them ... bake bread. I am not sure under the circumstances who will be the most punished.[9]

Among the notable internees were a son of Edmund Resch, the founder of the eponymous family brewery, and the manager of the Australian Metal Company, Franz Wallach, who came to Australia in 1893. After being formally denaturalized by his own country Wallach was naturalized in 1898. Under the War Precautions Act, the AMC had been declared an enemy company. Wallach appealed unsuccessfully through the courts to have the interment ban lifted.[10]

The case of Sydney orthopaedic surgeon Maximilian Hertz resonates as much for its professional jealousy as it does for anti-German sentiment. Born in Bochum, Germany, in 1876, Hertz, an outstanding medical student at the Friedrich Wilhelm University, Berlin, went on to become a leading orthopaedic surgeon. He arrived in Sydney in 1910 with his Australian wife and set up a surgery in Macquarie Street (Sydney's equivalent of London's Harley Street). His success in treating sufferers from bone deformities, twisted spines and other congenital conditions and infantile paralysis had his surgery crowded with patients. At the start of the First World War Hertz became a naturalized citizen. However, this did not give him protection against a sudden outburst of anonymous insults and abuse over his phone and through the mail. Despite the hostility, in May 1915 Hertz sought permission to establish a special orthopaedic hospital for soldiers suffering from war injuries. Failing that he offered his services to any department set up for soldiers needing orthopaedic surgery.

Instead he was arrested and interned at Holsworthy. In January 1916 he was transferred to the Trial Bay internment camp on the northern coast of New South Wales. When the Swiss consul Mark Rutty visited the camp he found the 580 inmates enjoying a holiday existence. They swam daily on the white sandy beach below the camp. They had access to a large library and hospital and had set up an orchestra and theatre. Hertz had been appointed camp medical officer and general medical practitioner for the district and was free to come and go. In an attempt at freedom he wrote to the Defence Department claiming under Article Nine of the Geneva Convention that he was a member of the German Army Medical Corps and should be given passage to Germany. The department rejected his plea. When Germany asked the British Government to repatriate twenty highly esteemed German-born men from empire countries, Hertz was tenth on the list. Australian Prime Minister Billy Hughes refused the request.

With the Armistice in November 1918 and despite the pleas of thousands of invalids all over Australia, Hertz was kept in custody. During that time his citizenship was revoked. It was not until April 1920 that the PM approved the doctor's release. He returned to his practice to find queues of patients. He decided to treat returned servicemen without charge – as he had always done with needy patients. However, operating theatres and wards of the major hospitals were closed to him due to the ongoing intrigues of other doctors. The Society of Returned Medical Officers and the British Medical Association New South Wales branch unsuccessfully campaigned for his deportation. As a result, in addition to reopening his old practice in Macquarie Street he set up a hospital at Rushcutters Bay, in central Sydney.

Hertz's knowledge, skills and experience were lost with his death in March 1948. Overworked and his health declining, he had tried to persuade other doctors to become a partner in his practice. But the enduring BMA ban stood in the way of anyone who may have contemplated doing so.[11]

Of the 6,739 men, sixty-seven women and eighty-four children interned in Australia during the war, fifty-eight escaped, 201 men and one woman died, 104 of these deaths being due to pneumonic influenza; 5,276, were deported in nine special ships, which sailed at various dates between May 1919 and June 1920.[12]

Despite the above details, the fact is the lives of most citizens identified as 'German' gradually returned to what they had been in pre-war years. A search for broad-ranging anti-German activities turns up scant material. Censorship is not to blame for this. As for the treatment of the internees, history professor Jürgen Tampke sums up:

> All told, the Australian authorities behaved well. They adhered to the Hague Convention that sets out that prisoners of war and other enemy subjects have to be treated with basic human dignity.[13]

The spy network

> Germans have shown they have no respect for any pledge however solemn and that the best cloak for a spy is British citizenship.
>
> *The Evening News*, London, 13 May 1915

For much of the war, Australian Defence Minister Pearce believed that Germany planned to invade Australia, a belief shared by many of his fellow citizens. Pearce further believed as part of Germany's plans, spies were operating in the country using hidden telegraph stations to transmit messages. The obvious place to find the spies was among those of German heritage. The minister was not an alarmist or a johnny-come-lately to the public domain. Born in South Australia in 1870, he settled in Western Australia, where he played a leading role in establishing the State's Trades and Labor (*sic*) Council and the WA branch of the Labor (*sic*) Party. In 1901 he became a senator in the first Federal parliament and retained this post until 1938. In 1908 he was appointed Minister for Defence and held the portfolio for practically all of the First World War.

In March 1917 Pearce approached the Chief of the General Staff, Brigadier-General H.J. Foster with his spying network suspicions. Foster reassured the minister, saying the director of military intelligence, Major E.L. Piesse, had told him there had been no case of spying since he took office in 1914.[14] Despite this reassurance, in the post-war years Pearce continued to maintain there had been a secret German war organization in Australia, although he never offered substantial proof to back his claim. Fischer describes the concept of German invasion and spying as a fantasy, adding, 'by the power of imagination and by wishful thinking ... Australians had managed to transport themselves into the centre of the war, from the distant periphery.'[15] Scott, writing in the 1930s, asserts, 'If there had been real spying [during the war], it is hardly likely those officers whose business it was to detect it would have failed to find instances.'[16] However, Heydon argues that Pearce's view of a conquest of Australia was consistent with the ambitions of the Kaiser.[17] It follows that a spy network would have been in place.

It was many years later before evidence was uncovered to show Pearce's suspicious were founded, in fact. It came about in 1987, when Jürgen Tampke was on a research visit to Germany. The University of New South Wales Associate Professor of History, who was then a senior lecturer in its history department, had finished examining files into German settlers in Australia in the nineteenth and early twentieth centuries and decided to take a routine look at military archives. The first on which he laid his hands sparked his interest. It was stamped '*GEHEIME AKTEN*' (secret file). Intrigued, he called for more files. These were stamped '*GANZ GEHEIM*' (extremely top secret).

It did not take him long to realize he had come across by chance evidence that a hitherto unknown German spy ring had operated in Australia prior to and during the First World War. The German-born, Australian-educated academic concluded that he had in his hands evidence that senior Australian public servants, businessmen and local Germans were involved in the ring. In an interview with me for a story I wrote for *The Daily Telegraph*, Sydney, Tampke said his findings overturned the long held 'fantasy' concept of a spy ring. He said:

> When Hughes [prime minister] warned the Australian people to be on guard for German spies he had reason for whipping up anti-German hysteria. The fact the government was largely ignorant about the identity of the German spies placed it in an awkward position. It was essential to stop enemy activity but with little specific knowledge the government had to embark on indiscriminate investigations and arrests. Certainly, as so often in history, innocent people copped the worst injuries.

Cautious in his observations he made the point that he had not foreseen the amount of interest the files had generated. He did reveal they showed the spy network in Australia had operated since 1890. The network was known in Berlin as the Australische Station, its secret headquarters was the Imperial German Consulate, Sydney. Here, until the outbreak of war, the information gathered by agents was collected, coded and transmitted to German naval ships that called regularly into Sydney. The ships passed on the messages by Morse code to the Chief of the German Admiralty, Berlin. The encoded messages were supposed to have been destroyed once read. But, as Tampke said, that was his second surprise, finding the messages had not been.

Tampke produced a file from the Sydney Vice Consul, in which he told Berlin that his spies, by bribing senior public servants, had obtained classified military maps from the Defence Department showing fortifications already built and those under construction along Sydney's coastal regions. The Vice Consul says he intends to obtain copies of plans for individual fortifications and discusses payments to those due to provide the information. Another report gives a detailed breakdown of Australia's military strength, while others discuss local ports at which coal might be obtained – by force of arms. For example, one port targeted for a possible coal raid was Gladstone, on the central Queensland coast. A blockade of Sydney and Melbourne by German armed cruisers was countenanced. Tampke said:

> They collected and collected whatever they regarded as relevant. [He produced a thick file of the top-secret papers.] It contains information that could not have been provided from Germany. The Germans amassed an immense amount of information for their warships. Its commanders knew of remote inlets and bays suitable for shelter and for launching surprise attacks. They were informed of the size, shape, firing range and other capabilities – and deficiencies – of Allied warships. They knew about the stationing of troops and artillery and of unprotected coal depots that could be destroyed or made use of. Maps indicated safe passages for submarines in the waters of the Great Barrier Reef. How well equipped they were with information can be seen by the journey of the *Emden*.

The *Emden* was part of Germany's Far East Squadron, which, as Tampke's documents reveal, had been preparing for years to carry out unrestricted warfare on shipping should a war start and Australia not remain neutral. Within the first three months of war being declared, *Emden* had sunk or captured twenty-four Allied ships, seriously disrupting the trade routes between Australia and Britain.

Its luck ran out on 9 November 1914. Wireless operators on board the Australian Navy cruiser HMAS *Sydney*, at sea in the Indian Ocean, picked up messages in a strange code. In the meantime, Australia's Cocos Island base reported an unidentified warship approaching. *Sydney* broke off its task of escorting the first European war-bound troop convoy to investigate. The appearance of the Australian ship on the horizon took the *Emden's* captain, Karl von Müller, by surprise. Although he put up a fight, von Müller was forced to surrender. The surviving members of his crew – 134 had been killed – were taken prisoner but not before they had destroyed confidential papers. Tampke feels that had Australian officials captured the papers, they would have exposed the German spy network in the Australian region.

In his book *Ruthless Warfare*, Tampke argues against the tendency of historians to question Australia's involvement in the First World War. His intention in publishing the spy files was to disprove the case that 'imperialists' in Australia and London manipulated the Australian people into supporting a war that was of no relevance to them. He says German warships in the Indian and western Pacific oceans were expected to make a significant contribution to Imperial Germany's confrontation with the British Empire to achieve its goal of a leading world power (*Weltmacht*). He quotes Hans Garpow, the senior officer of the Australian station, as reporting to the German Admiralty a plan to carry out ruthless warfare against Australia, in particular against its harbours.[18] The book justifies the professor's argument that because of the war intelligence system operating in the region, the internment of German nationals 'was not simply an unnecessary and unwarranted act of xenophobia and war hysteria.'[19]

On the other hand, in *Enemy Aliens*, published before Tampke's book, Fischer argues the arrest, internment and post-war deportation of German businessmen under the Trading with the Enemy Act had nothing to do with the war or spies but was part of a long-term strategy by Prime Minister Hughes to clear Australian industry and commerce of a German influence and tie them to Britain. As a result, innocents suffered.[20] McKernan cites Oscar Plate as one of those 'innocents'. Plate was a long-time Sydney resident and an employee of the Norddeutscher Lloyd Steamship Company.[21]

In May 1915 the *Daily Mirror*, a brash newcomer to the Sydney newspaper market, said of Plate:

[He] is still at large and enjoys the hospitality of this city at his beautiful home at Elizabeth Bay whilst his countrymen are poisoning our brave men in the trenches and are sending innocent women and children to destruction on the high seas ... This Hun can view every transport that leaves Sydney Harbour in comfort from his own verandah ... this representative of the nation of baby-killers can obtain an excellent view of Garden Island (naval dockyard) from his bedroom window ... The only safe place for Herr Plate is in Holsworthy concentration camp, or some equally secluded abode, where a bayonet or bullet will prove effective if any mischief is attempted.[22]

McKernan says the article was typical of the *Mirror's* anti-German attitude, noting the newspaper made no specific charges of disloyalty but combined opportunity and 'Germanism' to allege disloyal, treacherous action. He ridicules the newspaper's claim that authorities had traced stolen valuable documents to a former Sydney-based German consul general who had 'the means of furnishing' the German Pacific fleet with coal, wireless apparatus and so on. In this and other articles he says the *Mirror* was guilty of 'gutter tactics'; the impression it left was that it was written by cranks.[23] Based on Tampke's revelations, the newspaper's claims had substance. On the surface its comments on Plate are vitriolic and libellous. But the *Mirror* is not concerned he would sue. It appears it knew what Tampke's secret documents confirmed: Watching – and noting – shipping movements from his well-placed verandah was what Plate was doing for his Berlin bosses. The German Government had recruited Plate and another businessman, Otto Bauer, as Berichterstatter/Vertrauensmänner (informant/confidant). They were spies. When recruited both men had sworn on oath to work for the German Imperial Marine intelligence system and preserve its secrets 'to the utmost'.[24] Other BE/VMs reported from Fremantle, Adelaide, Melbourne, Brisbane and Auckland to the chief of the Australian network in Sydney. 'Documents do not support the view there was no real need for [the Trading with the Enemy] Act,' Tampke says. 'BE/VMs were responsible for gathering information of general and specific military use. The number of informants used by the BE/VMs in their work has remained an open question.'[24]

Neither Pearce nor the intelligence services had access to the damning documents contained in Tampke's book and nothing has surfaced in Australian Archives files to suggest intelligence sources acted on more than suspicions of the extent, or the existence, of an Australian station. As a consequence, in the intervening years the argument has prevailed that a mixture of jingoism, commerce and bias were the reasons driving the government in its anti-German actions.

Historian Robert McGregor finds validity in Tampke's contention that Germany posed a threat to the Australia-New Zealand region. He points out that other historians have given scant attention to the role of Pacific naval strategy in the First World War, in comparison to that given to Australian Army forces. This is reflected in current school history syllabuses. The First World War had come close. Australian and NZ forces occupied German territories in the Pacific and New Guinea while the *Emden* demonstrated there had been an immediate danger to Australia. He goes on:

> Given the race for arms and empire between Germany and Great Britain in the pre-war period … it seems inevitable that the Australia-New Zealand area would be included as part of a wider imperial grand strategy. German plans for dominance in the region were largely foiled by the arrival of the Australian fleet in 1913, while Japan's declaration of war against Germany left vulnerable the Imperial Fleet's only Pacific base. Australia was ready for war, impounding twenty-six merchant ships that Germany had planned to use as supply and support vessels for the German fleet.

The documents uncovered by Tampke, McGregor adds, should be of immense importance to both military and non-military historians as they reveal the German military also regarded the potential value of Australia and NZ in cultural terms.[25]

No man or woman was shot, hanged or otherwise executed as a spy or a traitor in Australia, nor was an Australian soldier executed for desertion.

Chapter 5

Shell-shocked

On 16 November 1915, both the 1st and 2nd Sportsman's battalions set out for the battlefront. Schwarz was left behind, still on the roll of the 30th Reserve Battalion, in billets at Leamington Spa. As the two battalions were landing in France Schwarz was taking part in the drill and bayonet fighting course, from which he emerged boasting, 'I obtained the highest number of marks in my class and was awarded a good certificate.'

His course completed, he returned to the Leamington Spa billets, where he was promoted to the rank of corporal. He says he applied many times to be sent to join the 1st, but was unsuccessful. However, unlike his experience in the AIF, he had no doubts his pose as a young Englishman would see him in action eventually. The 30th was originally formed to become the 3rd Sportsman's Battalion to take the overflow of applicants from the two other battalions, until somebody pointed out that a reserve force was going to be needed to replace the inevitable casualties.

Once in France the two battalions had been separated into different divisions. However, the men from both were gradually acclimatized by being placed in the trenches in small groups with more experienced soldiers for up to four days at a time. Here they found conditions far from those on the green playing fields of public schools or sporting grounds. It was winter and mud in the narrow trenches was above their knees, the dugouts leaked and their army issue boots did not keep their feet dry. The first casualty came on 5 December, when a 1st Battalion man was killed in a shelling. Two days later, a shell killed two other men from the 1st who comprised a machine-gun crew. The number of deaths and injuries was to increase as the battalion became more involved in front-line duties.[1] The 1st's initial experience as a unit in the trenches came when it took over a section of the front line in the town of Cambrin to relieve the Royal Berkshires.[2] Their trench was less than 1,000 yards (just over 900m) from the front. They had marched there on 19 December in pitch darkness and pouring rain. The effort was so hard they did not notice the sound of the guns drawing ever closer and were happy when star shells burst because it gave them light.[3] Older hands cursed those lights, particularly if it exposed them in the killing fields of no-man's-land on a night raid.

Christmas Day found the battalion still at the front and under an artillery bombardment that took its deadly toll.[4]

Relieved early in the New Year, the survivors' much needed rest was interrupted by a constant round of kit inspections, drills and route marches.[5] In February, Lieutenant Colonel H. Vernon, from the King's Royal Rifles, assumed command of the 1st.

Weeks later came the moment for which Schwarz had prayed and plotted: On 14 March 1916 he was listed in a draft to the 1st (also known by now as the 23rd Royal Fusiliers). The young Queenslander had shown himself to be a competent soldier and a leader among a group of men, many of whom were considered to be British officer material largely based on backgrounds unlike his of humble – and Germanic – roots.

With other draftees his records show he crossed to France on 15 March. As mentioned earlier, his memory of dates at times differs from official records. He says he joined the battalion on approximately 10 March. We do know it was to be another week or so after landing in France before he reached the front line, spending the preceding days at the 33rd infantry base at Étaples, a fishing and commercial port near Boulogne in the north of France, in the department of Pas-de-Calais. Étaples, on the right bank of the estuary of the Canche, is 4.5 kilometres from the Straits of Dover. Its population in the years immediately prior to the outbreak of war in 1914 was about 5,000, including a colony of artists. In the First World War the town became a military camp and hospital city for Australian, New Zealand and British casualties. Despite its position it was not a backwater of the war. German aircraft bombed camp and hospital. Today, Étaples is the site of a military cemetery containing more than 2,000 graves.

When Schwarz joined it, the 23rd was holding a section on the eastern side of the infamous Vimy Ridge. He found, in the short time they had been in France, his comrades – those high profile sportsmen and entertainers from public schools and universities, those gentlemen of leisure, who had joined in a blaze of publicity – were well on their way to becoming battle-hardened veterans of the British Army's 2nd Division.

The Germans had taken Vimy Ridge from the French in 1915. For much of the rest of the war it was one of the most dangerous sections on the Western Front. The British soldier in 1916 approached it from across a stretch of 2 to 3 miles of deceptively peaceful-looking countryside. Although its height was not great it dominated the landscape and grey smoke from shellfire constantly shrouded it. At night flashes of shell bursts lit up the area. Strategically it was regarded as of paramount importance and neither side was willing to cede the ground they had won or defended at great loss. Frank Watts, of the 15th Battalion London Regiment, was in the trenches that ran roughly parallel to the ridge at the time Schwarz arrived and was, like Schwarz, a corporal; both were to obtain commissions. Watts tells of an unsuccessful attack in which he took part. It began with men stumbling through darkness over the gentle rise leading towards the main ridge as shells whistled overhead. In no-man's-land, enemy flares rose to throw a sickly green light over the landscape and machine-gun bullets began to find their marks. Watts and another man dived into a shell crater. A rocket burst above them into three red lights – a German signal from the trenches to its artillery that the British were attacking. Watts goes on: 'Bits of steel hummed over us and dirt seemed to fall in showers. How long it went on I do not know.' More than 100 men from his company had gone into the attack. Less than fifty made it back to the shelter of their trenches as the attack faltered. Next day at dawn Watts found a friend lying face downwards in the bottom of his trench. He had a gaping hole in his back. 'I tried to move him; he groaned piteously ... and begged feebly for a drink.' The horror continued for Watts. That night he came across a headless corpse 'sitting alone in a shallow dugout ... How a headless corpse could be in that position and that place I could not imagine'.[6]

Since the Western Front had fallen into the near stalemate of opposing trenches by the spring of 1916, both British and German forces used tunnellers, mostly men who had been miners in civilian life, to dig beneath the facing trenches and set mines. The resulting explosions caused heavy casualties, confusion and panic. A report from the German 163rd Regiment when it was defending Vimy Ridge describes the hopeless feelings this evoked in the ordinary soldier:

> One stood in the front line defenceless and powerless against these fearful mine explosions. Against all other fighting methods there was some protection – against this kind of warfare valour was of no avail ... like lightning from the clear heavens, like the sudden occurrence of some catastrophe of nature these mine explosions took place ...[7]

The 23rd Battalion's war diary notes the following up to the time Schwarz was put on the boat back to England:

> 25 April 1916: Battalion relieved in trenches in Souchez 2 Sector by 1st King's Royal Rifle Corps and proceeded to billet in Bouvigny.
>
> 26–28 April: In billets in Bouvigny, providing working and carrying parties.
>
> 29 April: Battalion relieved 1st King's Royal Rifle Corps. On the left, the 2nd Ox and Bucks Light Infantry, on the right, the 1st Berkshire.
>
> 1 May: In the trenches. Received draft of 1 officer and 60 other ranks.
>
> 3 May: Battalion relieved by King's Royal Rifle Corps, and proceeded to billets in Bois de Noulette.
>
> 7 May: Battalion relieved by King's Royal Rifle Corps.

It was while the battalion was in the trenches (1 May) that Schwarz suffered what an initial casualty report describes as 'multiple but superficial wounds to his arms, legs and face'.[8] His wounding is not noted in the terse diary notes. According to First World War researcher Chris Baker, so commonplace had losses become during the battalion's tour of trenches between 29 April and 3 May, they were not recorded. Schwarz's medical notes show he was moved back along the casualty chain to the Number One General Hospital at Étretat before being shipped to England on the hospital ship *Panama* on 7 May. He was taken to Voluntary Aid Organization's Number Five Temporary Hospital, Exeter, where his record shows he was treated for seventeen superficial wounds – 'and shell shock'. He spent forty-two days at the VAO hospital, followed by three weeks at North Bovey Manor, Moretonhampstead. Soldiers of both world wars remembered the impressive looking manor house as a place in which they both convalesced and received treatment. Today the site is a hotel and golf club. What was the young pretender's reaction to his first taste of war? Laconically, he notes, 'I'm afraid that my work on that tour was practically nil.' In fact, Schwarz had done no fighting in the weeks he had spent in the war zone. He had been physically wounded. Both the wound and the reality of war had left him shell-shocked. In his petition to the king, Schwarz says he had been both 'badly wounded' and 'badly shocked', despite the official record describing his physical wounds as superficial.

It was the latter injury, however, that comes as a surprise, as much for the fact that he admits to it at a time when it was considered an excuse for 'shirkers' as for the fact it does not appear on a later document detailing his medical history up to 26 April the following year. Professor Charles Myers, a psychologist and captain in the Royal Army Medical Corps, coined the term 'shell shock' in 1914, believing its cause to be a result of physical injury to the nerves of a combatant caused by exposure to heavy bombardment; in other words, an organic cause. The term spread as rapidly as the number of cases reported. By 1916, more than 40 per cent of the casualties in fighting zones were victims and by the end of the war more than 80,000 cases had passed through medical facilities. Professor Joanna Bourke says victims were not shown sympathy; sufferers had to accept this injury damaged their reputations as both soldiers and men. She quotes an un-named British general: 'Other things being equal, the frequency of shell shock in any unit is an index of its lack of discipline and loyalty.' This was a widely held view and it made the burden of guilt for victims worse. The symptoms included hysteria, paralysis, blindness, deafness, limping, vivid nightmares, insomnia, hallucinations and memory loss. Others developed permanent psychiatric conditions, including schizophrenia and chronic depression. Suicide among its victims was not uncommon.[9]

The treatments for shell shock varied. Doctors put the stress on quick cures, as the goal of wartime psychiatry was to keep men fighting. Discipline was at first the most common treatment. Other methods were tried without lasting success including shaming, physical re-education and electric shock therapy. Another form of treatment consisted of finding out the likes and dislikes of patients and ordering them to apply themselves diligently to the latter.

What the generals and others committed to pursuing the war on both sides were loath to admit was the cause of the condition. It was simple and horrible, as Wendy Holden points out:

> War on the Western Front was different from any war fought before ... The nerve-shattering properties of the new killing machines ... aeroplanes, tanks and rapid-firing heavy calibre artillery brought mental resistance to saturation levels ... the British forces were continually harried and suffered heavy casualties ... Men had an average of four hours' rest per day and became mentally weak from the continual strain of being in the range of the relentless German guns ... The spirit-sapping mud, rain and freezing conditions in the trenches further compounded the misery, adding to the sense of ... helplessness and giving rise to mental desolation surpassing all previous experience.[10]

At the time Schwarz was diagnosed as a victim, twenty hospitals especially set up for the purpose to take the strain off military hospitals were treating shell-shocked patients. North Bovey Manor was one of those hospitals. It was not until 1917 that official attitudes began to change. Enlightened doctors re-diagnosed the condition as a temporary psychological breakdown brought about by the strain of war.[11] Modern armies go to war with psychiatrists as part of their armoury to deal with post-traumatic stress disorder (PTSD), which presents as similar to the shell shock of the First World War without the guilt.

The symptoms Schwarz displayed are not recorded. His neurosis may have been a delayed reaction. From his own admission he had been 'badly shocked'. Electric shock therapy may have been recommended.

He may have fallen into the hands of an enlightened doctor, possibly a Freudian ahead of the trend who treated him for a neurotic condition through psychotherapy. Once again, the passage of time prevents us knowing the details.

In his absence, the 1st was involved in one of the bloodiest engagements of the war. It began on 27 July, when they were heavily shelled at Bernafay Wood while, on their way to join the fighting in Delville Wood. Among the fatal casualties was the famous sculler William Albany. The battle for possession of Delville Wood in northern France had been raging since 14 July and was one of the early engagements in the Somme campaign. Fighting had settled into the capture of small strategic towns, woods or other features from which to direct artillery fire or to launch further attacks. Delville Wood, to the north-east of the town of Longueval, was one of those critical objectives for both German and Allied forces and resulted in heavy casualties on both sides. In Delville Wood, first into battle on the Allied side was the South African 1st Infantry Brigade. It was the brigade's first taste of warfare and a tragic one; it suffered losses of 80 per cent yet it managed to hold the wood until relieved by British forces, among them the 1st Sportsman's.

As they moved into the trenches on the edge of the Delville Wood the Sportsmen came across the result of hot weather and the earlier fierce fighting between the German and South African soldiers – unburied bodies. At 07.00 am on 27 July, the 2nd Division of the 99th Brigade, which included the 1st Sportsman's, the 22rd Royal Fusiliers, the 1st Royal Berkshires and the 1st King's Royal Rifle Corps, attacked. The Sportsmen charged under enemy artillery on the edge of the wood and into sputtering machine-gun fire as they entered the wood. In this initial confrontation an officer and twenty-six Other Ranks were killed and 143 wounded, while twenty men were listed as unaccounted for. Despite these losses the men took over a trench in the middle of the wood and held it throughout the day under an artillery barrage and fighting off counter-attacks. Among the casualties was another well-known sporting personality in civilian life, the boxer Jerry Delaney. Before being relieved on 29 July when the survivors returned to Bernafay, there had been nearly 400 casualties, 60 per cent of the men who had gone into the woods two days earlier. Out of eighteen officers, thirteen were casualties.

Overall, the 2nd Division force managed to clear a large area of the southern part of the wood and hold it until 4 August, when they were relieved by the 17th Northern Division. Michael Foley, author of *Hard as Nails*, the Sportsman's battalions' story, writes there was a 'strange' lack of publicity as to the 1st's part in the battle. Most publicity went to the South Africans.

Later in the month, the Germans counter-attacked across the now treeless terrain. Rain had turned the shell holes into swampy pools in which decaying bodies floated while other corpses lay half-buried in mud. The final German forces were driven from the wood on 3 September 1916.[12]

Following his convalescence and whatever psychiatric or other treatment doctors recommended, Schwarz was posted back to the 30th Reserve Battalion. By this time it was stationed at Leith Fort, near Edinburgh, Scotland. The likelihood of a recovering shell-shocked victim being sent once again into battle was not great, particularly if the victim had been diagnosed as incurable.

In Leith, Schwarz was appointed to the battalion's physical training staff. He could have sat out the rest of the war as a staff man. But this option did not suit him. A month in the front line, exposed to its barbarities and coming to a realization that the odds of escaping death, mutilation or madness were slim would have satisfied the conscience of many a man that he had done his bit for king and empire. Not Schwarz, who believed he had not seen enough active service. A cynic may suggest this proved he was still suffering from shell shock.

However, the battalion was in desperate need of reinforcements, as were all Allied divisions. Any man who wanted to go back did not have to use undue persuasion. In the process, 'shell shock' somehow disappeared from his later medical record and possibly the record of others who wanted to return to hell on earth.

Chapter 6

Monarch and Monash

From their first meeting a close rapport developed between King George and General Sir John Monash, the brilliant commander of Australian forces on the Western Front. As an expression of his regard for Monash, George, in a rare and ancient tribute, knighted the general in the field. Like Schwarz, both king and general suffered as a result of the German blood that ran through their veins.

Monash

While Schwarz at the lower end of Australia's military structure was complaining that his heritage was causing him to suffer humiliation, at the other end, Sir John Monash, who was to become Australia's greatest wartime commander, was suffering slights and barbs from fellow officers, citizens and politicians. Monash's heritage was Prussian-Jewish. His father Louis was the fourth of ten children who had emigrated from his birthplace, Krotoschin, Prussia, to Australia in 1853 intending to seek his fortune on the goldfields. Instead he joined a firm of softgoods importers. Towards the end of 1862 he returned home on a business trip, combining it with a visit to relatives. There he met and married Bertha Manasse, the sister of his brother's wife. The couple arrived in Melbourne on 5 June 1864.

Coincidentally, there is confusion over the birth date of both Schwarz and Monash. As we have seen, Schwarz's birth date when he enlisted with the AIF was put down as 24-4-1896. His birth certificate gives the date as 17-4-1896. In Monash's army records, which he personally filled out, on his tombstone and on the memorial tablet at Scotch College, Melbourne, the dates are 27 June 1865. But his birth certificate shows he was born four days earlier. The certificate also says he was born at home in Rachel Terrace, West Melbourne. Rabbi Dr R. Brasch points out that Rachel is a Jewish name; the name is and has always been Richhill Terrace.[1] The rabbi says the mistakes could be put down to the excitement of a father at the birth of a son or his German accent confusing the register, except that at that time it was the beadle of the Jewish community who registered births.[2] John was their first child and only son.

In July 1884, Monash, an engineering student, became a part-time soldier, joining the Melbourne University Regiment as a private. In a passage that could as well describe Schwarz's attitude to his militia training Pedersen writes:

> Monash's hunger for promotion, combined with a childish delight in a dazzling uniform and the status inevitably bestowed upon its wearer, suggest that Monash did not take too seriously those who told him there would be no long-term advantages.[3]

Monash later shared with Schwarz the fact they became members of garrison artillery units (Monash did so as a part-timer). He was commissioned on 3 March 1887. He did not serve in the Boer War due to business and family reasons.

A colonel in 1914, Monash's first wartime job was head of Australia's censorship body. His official title was Deputy Chief Censor in the Department of the Chief of the General Staff. The job gave him the responsibility of censoring cable and newspaper reports throughout Australia and maintaining communications with his boss, the British Chief Censor, at the War Office in London. He held the job for a matter of weeks, finding it distasteful. One of the 'distasteful tasks' was his interning of a group of German scientists whom, as organizer of a conference of the Australian Association for the Advancement of Science, he had helped to bring to Australia.[4] The scientists joined the other German internees at the Trial Bay 'holiday' camp on the northern coast of NSW for the duration.

On 15 September 1914, Monash was appointed to command the 4th Infantry Brigade. He was aged forty-nine. As a result of this senior command appointment, the anti-German campaigners in the community focused on him. His critics alleged he had been born in Germany and his mother had encouraged him from a young age to speak German as a first language. He, in turn, had encouraged his children to be fluent German speakers. Serle says German may have been the predominant family language prior to his attending school and his spoken English as an adult did have a slight accent, of which he took pains to rid himself.[5]

Citizens attacked him in letters to the Defence Minister, George Pearce, and signed petitions protesting his appointment.[6] Pearce declared he was satisfied with Monash's loyalty, which brought down on him the wrath of the antagonists. The minister commented later: 'Had I listened to gossip and slander as I was urged to do, Monash would never have gone to the war.'[7] When the Military Board stopped commissioning men of 'foreign origin' Monash noted bitterly it had ended the careers of fellow senior officers and 'crowds of junior officers whose names are a sure and certain index of foreign descent'.[8]

Despite this, his status as a public figure prompted his Australian cousins, the Behrends, to use his name spelt in the German way, Monasch. Monash demanded they cease 'this unwarrantable impertinence before it was grasped by his many enemies who are only too glad to seize upon anything that may injure me'.[9] As with other German settlers anxious to integrate into the community, his father Louis had dropped the 'c' from the name and become a naturalized British subject.[10]

The anti-German campaign followed Monash overseas. One rumour at Gallipoli had him as a German spy and Major General John Gellibrand, later Sir John, a divisional commander at Gallipoli, recommended sending home members of the Australian force of 'foreign origin'. Asked by another high-ranking officer should that include Monash, he replied, 'Yes, if his men distrust him …'[11]

In late 1915 Lieutenant General Sir William Birdwood, from the Indian Army, commander of the Australian and New Zealand Army Corps (Anzacs) in the Middle East, wrote of Monash's 'alleged German proclivities' in a discussion on appointments of Australian officers to higher command. He noted:

Monash I regard as a man of very considerable ability and with good administrative powers, and I think would do capitally commanding a division in peace time. It was owing to the fact I was not, however, at all sure of his ability to do this, and to do full justice to the troops serving under him, that I felt I could not conscientiously recommend him as suitable in all respects to command a division in the field, when actually fighting the enemy. He has not shown that resolution which I believe is really essential, while ... there is, I believe, among a considerable number of the force a great feeling against him on account of what they consider his German extraction.[12]

As with Schwarz, once given the chance to prove himself, his 'German extraction' became a non-issue. In France he earned wide respect as a divisional commander. He was the best on the Western Front, according to British general Sir Walter Congreve.[13] Early in 1918 he was appointed commander of the entire Australian Corps. In that role his brilliant planning and leadership in the final battles of the war further enhanced his reputation.

Andrews points out that Monash had many British admirers. 'His stress on training, meticulous planning, use of every available technology, co-ordination of forces and his ability to picture the ground over which he fought were among the talents that made him stand out from other commanders,' says Andrews.[14] Schwarz, too, through his own conscientious approach to soldiering reflected the qualities of the man who could have been his leader. Souter comments in a remark that could apply to Schwarz, 'one suspects that Monash ... was propelled and steered through his youth by a formidable mother' [Bertha].[15] Brasch agrees: 'However much Scotch College did for him nothing could replace the influence exerted on the young boy by his mother.'[16]

Souter says Monash was in line to replace Sir Douglas Haig as commander-in-chief of all British forces. He bases this assertion partly on a comment in the war memoirs of Prime Minister Lloyd-George, a critic of Haig, who said: 'I have been told by men whose judgment I value the only soldier thrown up by the war on the British side who possessed the necessary qualifications to become commander-in-chief of the British armies in France was a Dominion general. But I knew nothing of this at the time.' In any case, Monash had no intention of stepping aside from his position as C-in-C of the Australian forces. By

1918 they comprised an army twice the size of those led by the Duke of Wellington or Napoleon.[17] A great commander of the Second World War, Field Marshal Lord Montgomery called Monash the best general on the Western Front in the First World War, adding that had Monash replaced Haig as C-in-C of the British armies, the war might well have been over sooner and with fewer casualties.[18]

Post-war, by the time Monash arrived home he had become a national monument. For years he was asked to address a wide variety of organizations, having to refuse more invitations than he could accept. He was constantly asked for help by those who had served under him and just as constantly gave it. He was involved in charities and was patron of organizations who sought the prestige of his name. He and Schwarz silenced their biased critics by their determination and their wartime deeds. Both men in their separate spheres were rehabilitated heroes who seemed not to carry resentments towards members of the prevailing Anglo-Celtic society who had once rejected them and now fought to embrace and claim them as their own.

While Schwarz's ambition had been thwarted by his injury, Sir John looked forward to building on his wartime reputation to the extent he would one day receive a viceregal appointment. He had disclosed this ambition to his wife in a letter written in March 1918:

> My Dearest,
>
> ... The day when state governors will be chosen from Australian citizens is rapidly approaching. When that day arrives the field of choice will be very limited. There will not be a great supply of otherwise qualified men, who are not disqualified by their political prejudices or careers, or by having been state officials, and so lost their independence. It is therefore a quite legitimate ambition for a man in my position and nothing like so difficult a job as commanding a division in the Field.[19]

Monash died on 8 October 1931, aged sixty-six, his governorship ambitions unfulfilled. The day of Australian-born citizens replacing British governors had not yet dawned. His death was nationally mourned.

Monarch

With the same alacrity with which he had pardoned Schwarz, King George V would have endorsed Monash for a viceregal position had a state or the Commonwealth Government proposed him. Andrews notes a 'close rapport' between the two men from their first meeting.[20] On 12 August 1918, George knighted the Australian general in the field in the presence of 100 men from each of the five Australian divisions,[21] a rare and singular privilege that harks back to the days of the warrior kings.

Monarch and general could have conversed in German as in English. The subject of their conversations could have been the problems caused by their mutual German heritage in wartime.

King George was born on 3 June 1865, the second son of Edward VII and Alexandra. He was the grandson of the German Prince Albert, Victoria's consort, and a cousin of the wartime kaiser. His wife, Mary, had spent much of her childhood in Germany and remained in contact with her German relations during the war. She was born Her Serene Highness Princess Victoria Mary Augusta Louise Olga Pauline Caledonia Agnes of Tec, the daughter of the impoverished Frances, Duke of Tec. She was a great-granddaughter of King George III and a first cousin once removed of Queen Victoria. That is, her mother was Queen Victoria's first cousin. George and Mary married in 1893 and he ascended the throne in 1910 to continue the House of Saxe-Coburg.

With the outbreak of war, the Germanic name of the king and his wife's ancestral links became an issue. Their majesties tended to ignore the discreet concern that reached their ears. However, as the war progressed criticism grew louder and bolder. On 29 April 1917, that day's *Sunday Pictorial* came out in defense of the king's pedigree. It asked editorially:

> Are we in danger of forgetting that George the Fifth is the son of Edward the Seventh? … true, his grandfather (Prince Albert) was a German – though not, thank God, a Prussian – and his ancestors, generations back, were men of German blood and speech; but are we to deny to the King of All the Britons – to this quiet, gentle, Englishman – the son of Edward the Great and Alexandra the Good – the consideration that we commonly

accord to the naturalized German of the day before yesterday? It is monstrous, revolting, unthinkable … One thing only can more firmly cement the bonds that bind the Empire of the Throne. Let the Prince of Wales [the king's son] lead a British bride to the altar. And let him delete *Ich Dien* [I serve] from his crest. If necessary let this be done at the bidding of Parliament.[22]

Two points from this commentary are worth noting. First, the naturalized German living in Britain and those born of German origin possibly from families that had lived there for generations, were not being given universal consideration, particularly by the Army. Second, the Prince of Wales, as he then was, did not oblige the country or the *Pictorial* by marrying as a patriotic gesture. When he did marry years after the war it was not to a local lass but to American divorcee Mrs Wallis Simpson, after abdicating as King Edward VIII.

By mid-1917 the pressure on the king to establish his British credentials with a significant gesture proved to be too great to ignore. He was persuaded to do what Schwarz did, change the family name, with the obvious difference that George's had been inherited from Prince Albert. Alternatives considered with an Anglo ring to them included: Tudor, Stewart, Plantagenet, York, Lancaster and England. George decided on the suggestion of his private secretary, Lord Stamfordham: 'Windsor'. The new name was officially announced on 18 July 1917 in the following communiqué:

We, of Our Royal Will and Authority, do hereby declare and announce that as from the date of this Our Royal Proclamation Our House and Family shall be styled and known as the House and Family of Windsor, and that all the descendants in the male line of Our said Grandmother Queen Victoria who are subjects of these Realms, other than female descendants who may marry or may have married, shall bear the said Name of Windsor.

And do hereby further declare and announce that We for Ourselves and for and on behalf of Our Descendants and all other descendants of Our said Grandmother Queen Victoria who are subjects of these Realms, relinquish and enjoin the discontinuance of the use of the degrees, styles, dignities titles and honours of Dukes and Duchesses of Saxony and Princes and Princesses of Saxe-Coburg and Gotha, and all other German degrees styles, dignitaries, titles, honours and appellations to Us or to them heretofore belonging or appertaining.

While the king had been prevaricating over calls for him to give up his family name, the German heritage campaign had cost his cousin and friend, Prince Louis of Battenberg, his position as Britain's First Sea Lord. German-born Battenberg, who had wanted a naval career from a young age, had moved to Britain forty years earlier because the German Navy was then too small to offer him an opportunity to fulfil his dream. On 29 October 1914, the king wrote in his diary:

> Saw Winston Churchill [then First Lord of the Admiralty] who informed me that Louis … had resigned … The Press and Public have said so many things against him being born a German and that he ought not to be at the head of the Navy, that it was best for him to go. I feel deeply for him: there is no more loyal man in the country.[23]

Following his resignation under pressure, he anglicized the family name, to Mountbatten (Berg being German for mount or mountain). His son, a 14-year-old sea cadet at the time, vowed he would one day become First Sea Lord to right what he and others considered the wrong his father had suffered.[24] He succeeded as Lord Mountbatten of Burma. In the Second World War he was Supreme Commander of the Allied Forces South East Asia and post-war the last Viceroy of India.

In a final act of submission to the anti-German campaign, the king, against his wishes, was persuaded to remove eight enemy Knights of the Garter from the Order and have their banners taken down from St George's chapel at Windsor.[25]

A coincidence, as Duke of York, George had been honorary colonel of the Royal Fusiliers. In 1901 the duke visited Schwarz's home state, Queensland. His major memory of that brief visit may have been of the unsuitability of his Fusiliers outfit in the heat and humidity. His biographer, George Arthur, records that in the state capital Brisbane, 4,000 troops paraded for his inspection. Thomas opines they must have congratulated themselves that their own broad-brimmed hats were more suitable to the occasion than the varied headgear of members of the royal party: 'The sun beat viciously down... and the duke must raise his Fusiliers' headdress more than once to wipe his brow.'[26]

During the war the royal couple visited the battlefields in Europe several times; on one visit George's horse rolled on top of him, breaking his pelvis. As a result of the injury he was in pain for the rest of his life. He died on 20 January 1936.

Chapter 7

A Knight's Wound

In August 1916 Schwarz was posted back to France to rejoin the 23rd Fusiliers. It was still a part of the by now battle-hardened 2nd Division. The division had lost many men since he was last in action. The 23rd was holding a section of the front between the Redan Ridge (near Beaumont-Hamel) and Hebuterne. Again, Schwarz has trouble at times with dates. In this case, he says he rejoined the battalion on approximately 24 September, when records show it was a month earlier.

On 21 September 1916, Schwarz notes his commanding officer, Colonel Vernon DSO, told him, 'He had good reports of my first tour of duty with the battalion and that I was promoted ... and was to take charge of a platoon of D Company.'

On 13 November 1916, the 2nd Division captured Beaumont-Hamel. British commanders wanted to exploit the success. However, winter was closing in and made further fighting impossible. Schwarz notes that having taken part in the attack, they held the line for some days. He goes on to say his commanding officer once more sent for him. 'Colonel Vernon ... informed me that he had recommended me for a commission and that I was to proceed to England to attend an Officers Cadet Battalion [OCB].'

Materially he would be exchanging the rankers' ill-fitting army issue uniform of cap, baggy tunic, webbing belt and trousers stuffed into puttees for a tailored uniform jacket, open at the collar to reveal a shirt and tie, crossed with a Sam Browne belt of polished leather and a peaked cap. Officers bought their uniforms from such places as Barker's Man's Shop in London's Kensington High Street. Schwarz had first stepped out in the capital in 1915 a discontented Anzac gunner in slouch hat and baggy uniform, required to salute men his age in their tailored dress. He had in his original persona posed for a photograph in his cadet officer's uniform, a teenager standing beside his seated and proud mother. He always believed one day he would again stand beside her as an officer. But under current circumstances how could he make it possible?

Winter says the first trademark of the British officer was his uniform. It was the civil equivalent of hunting dress. Riding boots and breeches marked remoteness from physical labour and the Sam Browne identified him as a member of the sword-bearing class.[1] From the moment he had donned the dress of an officer, albeit a cadet officer, Schwarz had comfortably conjured his natural status in life. The pioneer in self-image psychology Dr Maxwell Maltz writes: 'Numerous case histories have shown that one is never too young or too old to change his self image and thereby start to live a new life ... once the concept of self is changed, other things consistent with the new concept of self are accomplished easily and without strain.'[2]

Schwarz in this sense is a prime example of the doctor's reasoning. As we have seen he had done this before, changing his persona from that of a professional soldier named Walter Schwarz, a former grocery store assistant, the son of parents whose background was solidly Germanic, to that of Walter Merritt, the son of an Englishman, who had no military experience. Schwarz may have not been aware his change of identity had involved an unconscious personality change. But as a measure of his actions and motives we have some understanding of Schwarz's survival instincts under conditions that would have tested a lesser determined soul beyond breaking point. In the post-war era when circumstances required he changed again, he did not want to. But he did.

Schwarz was back in England on 9 December 1916. Here again, this date in his service record differs to the extent it needs noting from the date in his petition to the king: 'about 22 December'. The following day he began a furlough (leave) over the Christmas period. His address during the time until he reported back was 39 Beauchamp Avenue, Leamington Spa. As with many things forgotten in time we do not know with whom he stayed. With army friends? Possibly 39 was a guest house catering for men on leave.

On 3 January 1917 he reported to No. 7 Officer Cadet Battalion at Femoy, County Cork, Ireland. Until 1915, courses for officers had lasted one month, on the assumption candidates came from an 'officer class', having attended a public (that is, private) school and in addition had most likely trained in its cadet corps. As the need for more officers grew in proportion to their casualty toll the course was extended to three months to cater for men who were not finitely considered by class officer material and did not have a cadet corps background; Schwarz had such a background in Australia, but, naturally, he could not claim it. He had said in his enlistment papers he had no previous military experience. True as far as his alter ego 'Merritt' was concerned. Even so, the newly commissioned officer heading for the front line did not need Schwarz's military knowledge. 'All he was thought to need was "authority" … with rites of initiation to help the repudiation of an old identity, time to consolidate extra self-confidence and the support of the hierarchic army structure,' says Winter. He was considered to have qualified if he could 'take with him those appurtenances of distinction which marked the authority of a civilian gentleman'.[3]

Schwarz was able to show his superiors he had acquired the 'appurtenances', either learnt or innate.

Once again, Schwarz lets us know he was a high achiever. 'At a final interview, Colonel Williams (the cadet battalion commanding officer) informed me that I had done well in my examinations and that he had no hesitation in recommending me for a commission.' On 24 April 1917, 'I received my second commission, as a second lieutenant in His Majesty's land forces.' His record of service says he was commissioned into the territorial force, a mistake. He was appointed to the Regular Army. His name was among a long list of appointments and promotions announced in the supplement to *The London Gazette*, 16 May 1917. He was one of seven men from the Royal Fusiliers commissioned temporary second lieutenants.

Schwarz arrived back in France on 9 June 1917, and a week later was posted to the 2nd Battalion Royal Fusiliers (City of London Regiment), which was attached to the 29th Division. Officers appointed from the ranks were not returned to their old units. Instead they were sent to units where they were not known as former rankers. The 29th Division was one of those selected to be in the first assault of a major offensive by the British in an attempt to break out of the Ypres salient and recapture the Belgian coast. The 29th had three tours of operations during this offensive officially known as the Third Battle of Ypres and to the troops as 'Passchendaele'.

On 9 October 1917 the war diary of the 2nd Royal Fusiliers records it was involved in the assault on two strongholds named Conde House and Olga House. Research produced only the first two pages of a longer report on this operation, kept in the British National Archives. The other pages, including the casualty list, have been lost.[4] The surviving pages detail a typical story of a minor action in a mammoth war. The report notes that slippery ground and the large number of shell craters made the dawn advance difficult but 'not as bad as might be expected considering the weather'. Five minutes after zero hour an enemy barrage began and grew heavier, 'although it was never very formidable. The enemy seemed quick in following the attacking waves with his guns, but never seemed to quite get its target.' Near Conde House the advance came under severe rifle fire, resulting in twenty casualties, and the advance was brought to a halt as the men found shelter in shell holes. During this action Schwarz writes he was again wounded but remained on duty. Schwarz does not enlarge on this incident or offer more than the bare facts.

The next major Ypres offensive, Cambrai, has the distinction of being the first in which tanks were used in any number. It began on 20 November 1917 with a 100-gun Allied barrage. At the same time more than 370 British tanks began to rumble towards the Hindenburg line on a 6 mile (approx 10km) front, crushing barbed wire barriers and rolling over trenches. At the end of the day this section of the line had been overrun and 6,000 Germans had surrendered. More than 170 tanks had been lost. In a counter-attack on 30 November, the British, unable to call upon reserves to consolidate their position, were hurled back and within two days had lost the ground they had gained. They were able to hold their positions with the help of the remaining tanks.

The battle of Cambrai cost each side about 45,000 men.[5] The Royal Fusiliers' latter role in the counter-attack had been to defend the village of Marcoing. It put up a strong resistance, allowing other units of the division to withdraw through it in good order. Schwarz notes that for his involvement in Cambrai, and an earlier battle at Langemark, 'I believe I was recommended for a decoration as I received a divisional card of honour.' It was signed by Major General, Sir Beauvoir de Lisle KCB DSO, who commanded the 29th Division between August 1915 and 12 March 1918.

After Cambrai the 29th had two relatively quiet tours holding the new line near Passchendaele over the last winter of the war. Late in February 1918, Schwarz records, another senior officer sent for him, Brigadier General Cheape, commander of the 86th Brigade, to inform Schwarz he was to join his staff as brigade intelligence officer. It was a compliment to Schwarz's qualities in the field. The position required him to be alert at all times, to be able to interpret signals and messages verbal and written, to help and advise in plotting and counter-intelligence – and ensure plans did not fall into the hands of the enemy. Whether or not Cheape knew it, Schwarz's experiences in maintaining his own personal secrets made his an ideal appointment.

Although in its final year, the Allies still had to win the war. Earlier in the year the odds seemed stacked in favour of the Germans following the Russian Revolution, in which that country's new Bolshevist leaders made peace with Germany. As a result, Germany was able to withdraw divisions from its Eastern Front and send them west. On 21 March at 4.40 am, a German barrage of 6,000 guns signalled the start of a major offensive on the British armies from the Somme to Cambrai. The barrage gave way to the advance of sixty-two German divisions. By 26 March, the German advance began to fade and the British defences strengthened. A frustrated General Erich Ludendorff, the German commander, changed direction to the Lys front and on 9 April launched a second devastating attack aimed at the vital railway centre of Hazebrouck. The 29th Division was among those rushed into line to try to stem the advance. The fighting was in the open, across fields that had been behind British lines for some time. The First World War researcher Chris Baker notes farm buildings and villages in the area were in most cases standing, as were copses and fences. This was rare terrain in the wasteland of the Western Front. Over the next month the British defence held and the Germans advanced less than 5 miles (8km) before coming to a forced halt. Had they broken through they would have reached Dunkirk, bringing the cities of Calais and Boulogne within range of their guns.

Schwarz records he received his first decoration in the Lys battle, a mention in Field Marshal Haig's dispatches (MiD). However, it appears to refer to an action before the battle as it is dated 7 April 1918. There is further dispute about the date as it is also mentioned as being awarded on 28 May. The mention, which carries the 7 April date, came in the form of a certificate signed by the secretary of state for war and records it was awarded 'for gallant and distinguished service in the field'. It goes on: 'I have it in command from the king to record His Majesty's high appreciation of the services rendered.' Schwarz does not give any further details and none are shown on his record.

The next few months were relatively quiet for the 29th Division. Time was spent strengthening trenches, making small raids to probe the enemy's defences and training for future battles. Corporal C.R. Russell of the 1st/4th (City of London) Battalion (London Scottish) found duties had devolved into three-man units:

> One was on guard. One was cleaning up the trench and trying to improve it and the other one would be having a sleep and you'd swap around, so you got an hour's sleep out of three unless someone got the wind up, when you'd jump up and get on the fire-step … it didn't take long for us and the Jerry troops to say 'you keep quiet and I'll keep quiet'. Just an unspoken understanding.[6]

On the other hand, Private J. Bowles of the 2nd/16th (County of London) Battalion (Queen's Westminster Rifles) found the opponents in his section reached no such understanding. He recalls 'a terrible strafing' (ground attack involving bombing and machine guns) near his post.

> It was splendid to watch but as shrapnel fell within a yard or two, it was quite close enough to be unpleasant. The trench mortars are the things we most dread. They drop right into the trench, and if you are near you don't stand an earthly. … Whizz-bangs are small shells that don't give you time to say 'Jack Robinson'. All you hear is a whizz and a bang. You automatically duck but if it is near you it is of no avail. Oilcans are really old oil drums filled with high explosives and any rubbish they can put in

of a killing nature such as small pieces of iron, steel and broken bottles. You can see these coming in the daytime and, depend on it, we give them a wide berth. Sling-bombs, hand and rifle grenades are very similar to our own and don't do a great deal of damage unless one drops at your feet. The trench mortar shell is like a football on a stick. You can see them coming in the daytime and at night they are followed by a shower of sparks, so if you keep your eyes open, you have some chance of getting clear.[7]

Casualties had another cause at this stage of the war: a virulent Spanish flu epidemic. Schwarz did not succumb. Many weakened by their wounds did. It was a time before antibiotics.

Schwarz's temporary appointment as brigade intelligence officer had been made permanent on 4 August 1918. During an attack on Ploegsteert, Schwarz was awarded his Military Cross. Today Ploegsteert is known best for its First World War Memorial. It lies on the road between Armentières and Ypres and records the names of 11,447 men who fell in the battles of Armentières, Aubers Ridge, Loos, Fromelles, Estaires, Hazebrouck, Scherpenberg and Outtersteene Ridge as well as men who have no known grave. Ploegsteert Wood Cemetery contains 165 soldiers: 117 UK, twenty-eight Canadian, eighteen New Zealand, one Australian and one unknown grave.

Schwarz's award, posted in the supplement to *The London Gazette* of 11 January 1919, says:

> At a very critical moment when one battalion was completely out of touch with both flanks which had been held up, he readjusted the whole line under extremely heavy fire at close range and led troops into position, gaining touch with the advanced battalion and ensuring the safety of its flanks. Throughout the operation his courage and initiative was most marked.

On 28 September the division was involved in a major offensive designed once again to break out of the Ypres salient. The 86th Brigade advanced in heavy rain under machine-gun fire, not to mention artillery, gaining and holding ground. According to the brigade's report of operations, while leading the attack at its centre Schwarz wore a large red patch on his back and carried a red flag. 'This proved invaluable in assisting troops to keep proper direction,' the report notes. Schwarz explains he wore the patch and carried the red flag because the area to be crossed by the brigade was devoid of landmarks. He positioned himself in the centre so that he could easily be seen by troops on either flank as well as those in the following waves. In other words, he was keeping the attackers on course. A British officer was a distinctive target in his 'hunting outfit'. An officer who further identified himself by carrying a large flag provided a compelling target. Whether he volunteered for the task – and his undoubted courage makes this likely – or it was a matter of duty as brigade intelligence officer to carry it, he was recommended for a bar to his Military Cross. It was not awarded. He did receive a second MiD from Field Marshal Haig.

The practice of carrying a regiment's pennant into battle had fallen from favour, one reason being its carriers were most likely to end up in the same position. The brigade's official report of the operation says the advance was stalled as a result of 'the enemy resistance having been strengthened'.

On 5 October, the division moved into advanced positions near Ledeghem, Belgium, another town that today has a war graves cemetery, its main attraction for tourists. In October 1918 it was a well-built town with a population of 9,000, set in low-lying country. It survived hardly touched until late in the war. The Allies captured it on 11 October, a few days before Schwarz was to fight in his last battle to the east of Ledgehem. On 14 October, as the soldiers were moving into position on the eve of this attack, in England British Prime Minister David Lloyd-George was wondering prophetically at an unofficial gathering of British and American politicians and senior officers what effect an immediate ceasefire would have on Germany. 'Was it really worth stopping the fighting unless Germany was badly beaten?' he asked rhetorically, continuing:

What if the democratic government in Berlin ... did not last? The German public could then be told 'those miserable democrats had taken charge and had become panic stricken.' ... If peace were made now, in twenty years time the Germans would say what Carthage had said about the First Punic War, namely that they had made this mistake and that mistake and that by better preparation and organization they would be able to bring about victory next time.[8]

The morning of 14 October started out clear but was soon shrouded in fog made denser by British smoke shells. It hampered the vision of both attacker and defender.

The brigade intelligence report records it began the advance at 05.35. Once again, Schwarz was leading the first wave of the attack carrying the red flag, which had proved so valuable on 28 September. He and the men with him followed the British barrage as it stepped farther into enemy lines. They crossed no–man's-land and reached the first objective well ahead of the rest of the brigade, whose members were having difficulty in getting through Ledgehem owing to the dense fog. This put them in a tight spot. 'We found ourselves practically surrounded by the enemy. Although we were heavily engaged … at close range, with machine gun and trench mortar fire,' Schwarz writes, adding, 'we succeeded in holding the objective.' They more than held it. They captured twenty-eight prisoners. In what is almost an afterthought he relates that he was wounded. It was a serious injury; a bullet fired at close range smashed into his right leg, fracturing it. Despite this he kept the flag flying, ensuring the following troops maintained the line and swept through to rout the opposition.

To the rational mind making oneself an easy and obvious target is foolhardy. The conclusion, however, must be Schwarz's bravery and sense of honour – and self-image – drove him to put duty above self-preservation.

The official history of the 29th Division records the attack advanced throughout the day, breaking through a broad band of barbed wire that had been another reason for the temporary delay in the advance. By the end of the day it had overcome stout resistance at various points and overrun German gun battery after battery, capturing at least fifty weapons and more than 1,000 prisoners.[9]

The brigade intelligence report records the bare details of the incident that ended Schwarz's war: '2/Lieut. MERRITT. Bde I.O. wounded.'

Members of his family tell me Schwarz was left lying where he had been hit. This claim is supported by a contemporary, who wrote at the time, 'He had been in no-man's-land for so many hours that his leg had become septic.'

Had he been treated soon after being wounded his leg may have been saved.

As he lay on the battlefield clutching the flag, the young man, who had taken on the name of the noblest knight, may have found relief in his pain with the thought he was dying a soldier's death, a passing he had told his mother was the noblest of them all.

> *Through dust of conflict and through battle-flame;*
> *Tranquil you lie, your knightly virtue proved*

For this final act of gallantry he was recommended and received a Bar to his Military Cross.

The Military Cross

In the semi-biographical anti-war novel *Not So Quiet: Stepdaughters of War*, the middle-class mothers of a young British captain, Roy Evans-Mawnington, and his fiancée, Voluntary Aid Detachment (VAD) ambulance driver Helen Smith, are spending the First World War competing on committees that encourage young men and women to 'do their bit' by enlisting. Roy pleases both mothers by winning the Military Cross, at a cost. Wounded for the third time, as with Schwarz, his leg is amputated above the knee. Worse than Schwarz, he is blinded in both eyes. Her unit commander thinks she is sympathizing with Smith when she says 'he behaved with conspicuous bravery and is to have the MC, Smith, let that console you … A great honour. If you want to weep …' Smith, who has transported to hospital too many men suffering terrible injuries, who has lost her sister and fellow VAD drivers in enemy attacks, is beyond weeping. 'His mother will be pleased with the MC, ma'am,' is her terse response. Her mother writes, 'My Dearest Girlie, Isn't it wonderful and sad. Our poor blinded hero. Darling, what an inestimable privilege you have, marrying one of England's disabled heroes, devoting your life to his service!'

Her putative mother-in-law in her letter to Smith relates that he had held a trench when three quarters of his men were dead, until relieved. 'As soon as he is strong enough he goes to Buckingham Palace for the investiture – a great honour – and the king will personally thank him for his bravery ... He is, of course, a trifle depressed but that will wear off ... I thank God for blessing me among all women for mothering a hero, an MC.' Roy dictates a letter to Smith to tell her that the shell that blew away his leg also rendered him impotent. As a result he releases her from any obligation to him. He goes on, 'I suppose they've [the mothers] told you of the MC ... If I was writing this myself I'd tell you what they could do with it.'[10]

Instituted in December 1915, the Military Cross fulfilled the need for an officer's gallantry award lesser than the Victoria Cross or the Distinguished Service Order, the latter for majors and above. It comprises a silver cross with straight arms ending in broad finials decorated with imperial crowns. The royal cipher is placed at the centre, and the medal is suspended from a 38mm wide purple ribbon by a plain silver suspender. The reverse is plain, although since 1938 the date of the award appears on the lower reverse. Awards personally presented by the monarch are officially engraved on the medal. Private engraving of the reverse is fairly common. Bars to denote subsequent awards are also in silver and have the crown at the centre.

The MC was originally awarded to captains, lieutenants and warrant officers of the Army, including the Royal Flying Corps. Eligibility was later extended to equivalent ranks of the Royal Navy, Royal Marines and Royal Air Force and the equivalent forces from the dominions and colonies. In 1931 the award was extended to the rank of major. Since 1993, when the Military Medal, the equivalent award for the lower ranks, was discontinued, the cross has been awarded to service personnel from the rank of major downwards. At first recipients were not allowed to use the letters MC after their names to indicate their award, but this restriction was later withdrawn. Of the 37,081 MCs awarded for the First World War, 2,992 received one bar, six two, and four three.

Chapter 8

'I Would Liketono Were He Is'

In his seminal work on members of the Australian and New Zealand Army Corps (Anzacs) in the First World War whose ancestry was German, John Williams says it is doubtful Schwarz's mother was able to find out until after the war that her son was serving under an assumed name in a British regiment.[1] A 1985 article in the Brisbane *Sunday Telegraph* claimed, 'his secret life in the British Army was not known to the townsfolk of Toowoomba until August 1921 – six years after he deserted.'[2] Viewed in the light of these opinions the assumption is that Schwarz's actions were selfish; he realized but did not care they would spark consequences for his family and friends.

When word spread in Toowoomba that Schwarz had deserted, life did become uncomfortable for his widowed mother, Augusta (Minnie) Schwarz, and her other three children. In the community her son was talked about as a traitor, a spy. People snubbed the family, others made insulting, even threatening, remarks – a bullet was placed in the mother's letterbox.

Williams asks how could Schwarz have let his mother know what he had done when his mail, written under the name of Merritt, would have been subject to censorship? Williams cites as evidence of the mother's ignorance a letter she wrote on 15 January 1916 to the Department of External Affairs asking for information of her son's whereabouts. Williams describes her writing as 'spidery' and her grammar and punctuation as 'typical of Australians of German origin and upbringing at that time'.[3] She was born in Ipswich, Queensland. Her poor English grammar is either a criticism of the public education system at the time, or an indication she attended a German-speaking school before the Queensland Government shut them down. Her son's birth certificate shows her birth date as 1866, while family history records give it as 1868.

Her letter:

To the Department of External affairs
Dear Sir.

I been writing since to the old address as he told me perhaps that why I
don't hear from him would you Kindly try and find him for me for I would
liketono were [sic] he is. You will see by the letter I sent that he is in the firing
line some were he was thinking they were going to France, I don't believe
for one moment that he would leave his Ranks for he seem, so ansius to go
to the front

Please let me know as soon as can

Augusta Schwarz[4]

She 'sent', that is, enclosed, a letter from her son, with hers. It appears
to be the following letter that Schwarz wrote to her in September 1915,
while he was with the AIF 55th Battery at Lydd, Kent:

Dear Mother

I am not going up to the Big Smoke [London] to night [sic] so I will write you
a few lines. We had a shoot yesterday, and all being well and we can get our
guns we ought to be having a go at them by the time you get this. We had an
examination for Observers last week & I got third place out of our Battery.
The field glasses come in very handy when you are out on a days [sic] outing.
The Boys are all well and are very anxious to get to the front although we are
having a great time in England, we get the best of food and have good huts to
live in. I believe some of us have got to be left behind till the next lot there are
[sic] many of us. They say, that is the wounded Australians in London, who
have been at the Dardanelles, that you can get all the fighting you want there.
And if I had the chance I would gladly shoulder the old rifle again, and go
with the infantry for the simple reason that the Infantry have the brunt of the
fighting were [sic] as we are in the rear the whole time, and might never see
the enemy, but I suppose no matter where you are you are doing your share
and one corps is no good without the other

I suppose you have heard from me by now although I have only got two of
your letters. What do you think of the Post Cards of Westminster Abbey my
word I wish you could only see it in reality, it is just marvelous, every village

in England has a large church, about 800 years old so you can guess what they are like …

I was in London during one of the Zepplin [*sic*] raids, the rotters, they drop a bomb and then go for their lives, but before we are finished we will give them all the raids they need.

I suppose you have heard Will Jefferson is dead poor chap, he has at any rate died a Soldiers Death, which is I think the noblest death of all.

Well mother I will close with best love and may God keep you safe till I return.

Your loving Boy Les XXX. Best love and kisses to Minnie XX.[5]

Minnie was the younger sister. The other two children were William and Lily.

His thoughts of dying a 'Soldier's Death … the noblest death of all' reveals the persistence of the romantic streak that inspired him from an early age to take up arms, a sentiment that may have allowed him to ignore the reality of the situation in which he claimed in his petition he found himself. The hurt, he says, was caused by fellow soldiers and the officers. His comment 'Boys are well … we are having a great time in England, we get the best of food and have good huts to live in' appears as Schwarz's attempt to reassure his mother he is one of the boys and she should not worry about their living conditions. A reader of the letter who did not know the story Schwarz related in his petition would conclude an alienated soldier had not written it. One wonders whether he had at any time told his mother of the problems caused him by his German name since joining the Army. Or was he like the boarding school student who is reluctant to mention in letters to his parents he's being bullied – until matters come to a head and the boy takes precipitate action in an attempt to restore his equanimity? The most interesting line in the letter is: 'I believe some of us have got to be left behind till the next lot …' It is a plausible alternative to the discrimination he claims was stopping him from being sent into action. Army units do not initially commit their full force to battle, men are held in reserve for logical reasons, to replace the inevitable casualties, to train new recruits, to keep the home base operational, to protect and maintain equipment and handle supply lines … many reasons.

External Affairs replied to Mrs Schwarz on 29 January 1916 to say her letter had been passed on to the Defence Department. In its letter, Defence gave a woman who claimed ignorance of the whereabouts of her son no comfort or solace. It is terse and unsympathetic as befits a relative of a deserter:

Dear Madam,

I am in receipt of your letter of the 15th instant, and in reply have to state that your son, No. 256 Gunner W.L. Schwarz, 55th Batt., 'O' Siege Brigade, R.G.A., is posted as a deserter from the Australian Imperial Force as from 25.10.1915.

Yours faithfully
Capt.
Office i/c Base Records'[6]

Williams goes on to assert that Mrs Schwarz had no means of knowing he had joined the Fusiliers under an assumed name.[7] It is difficult to accept this for a number of reasons. Her letter was to External Affairs, an indication she knew he was no longer under the control of the Defence Department. Her words 'I don't believe for one moment that he would leave his Ranks ...' suggest she had heard that was what he had done. At times families first learnt a relative had deserted when police arrived on the doorstep.

Having assumed Schwarz's mother's ignorance, Williams offers this criticism: 'If the inevitable breakdown in normal family communications brought on by his changed circumstances worried Schwarz, he seemed to show little sign of it ... the life of an infantryman plainly agreed with him.'[8] Williams does say Schwarz had good reason for secrecy – desertion, he points out, was punished by death before a firing squad.[9] That crime was hanging over Schwarz's head when the king pinned the medal on the chest of Lieutenant Walter Merritt MC and Bar and shook his hand at Buckingham Palace. As far as we know His Majesty was unaware at the time of Schwarz's true identity. My research shows the resourceful Schwarz had found means of defying the censorship restrictions and he did keep his family and friends informed of his whereabouts and his activities while swearing them to secrecy. One possibility was the address he gave at the Fusiliers' recruit depot, 23 Warrender Road, Islington. Letters from this address, under the name of its tenant, Croucher, to Schwarz's friends back home would not have aroused suspicions of staff at the Toowoomba post office.

A reliable source in the argument for ongoing knowledge being received in Toowoomba of Schwarz's activities as Merritt is his cousin, Joyce Hampson, who says that during the war Schwarz 'often wrote to a friend in Toowoomba who passed his messages on to his mother to let her know he was alright [sic].' Note, he wrote to a friend, not his relatives, with whom he was close, or direct to his mother, with whom, as we have seen, he wrote regularly prior to his desertion. Unfortunately, Mrs Hampson, who died in 1996, did not enlarge on her claim.[10] A likely bet, the 'friend' was the person who revealed Schwarz's story in a letter to the *Toowoomba Chronicle* in 1921 and signed it with the nom de plume Fair Play. Attached to the letter was a copy of Schwarz's petition to the king, which Fair Play could only have received from Schwarz. Two copies of the petition are known to exist; one is held in the British National Archives and the other in the Australian War Memorial Collection. The latter copy was submitted by Mr F.H. Bradley, a nephew, who was given it by Schwarz's widow. Fair Play confirms Mrs Schwarz's suffered for years the venom of townsfolk. However, his letter includes the revealing statement: '... for five long years she had to keep silent ... while all the time we knew how nobly he was fighting.' This appears to be irrefutable evidence she and the 'friend' had knowingly carried the secret of his whereabouts since 1915 without either of them yielding to provocation. Schwarz may have arranged with Fair Play a means of communicating under the name he was to assume, or yet another name before he left Australia's shores. As he says in his petition, he deserted using 'plans already made' without saying when such plans had been drawn up. But we do know he complained of discrimination before leaving Australia.

While on the subject of letters it has to be kept in mind that even under the best of conditions mail took weeks to reach Australia from Europe. It came by sea. On occasion a letter from a Digger arrived after his relatives had been officially told of his death.

Fair Play goes on to say he has army documents to back up Schwarz's claims of the honours he won in battle, as well as wartime medical reports from the matron and sisters at No. 8 Stationary Hospital, Wimereux, France. One of these reports brought grim news: 'Very little hope was entertained of his pulling through.' Believing he was dying, Schwarz had passed on Fair Play's address to nurses. Fair Play writes in the 1921 letter he had 'wanted to move in the matter of clearing his [Schwarz's] name long ago, having sufficient material in my possession to do so.' Schwarz would not agree, not until he had seen 'the thing through'. In total his claims amount to strong proof Schwarz was in touch with his mother through him and that she had remained foremost in his thoughts. Who was Fair Play? Hiding behind a nom de plume was a judicious move given what he revealed rendered him liable to prosecution for not having done so during the war. A clue to his possible identity may be found in the *Toowoomba Chronicle* report on the civic reception given Schwarz on his return to Toowoomba: it says Schwarz was taken to the town hall ceremony in a car driven by 'an old comrade, Mr Bews'.[11] This was most probably Scottish-born William Bews, a Toowoomba blacksmith in civilian life. Bews was single when he enlisted in September 1916 aged twenty-six. He sailed for Europe in May 1917 as a sapper with the 14th Field Company Engineers and returned home to Toowoomba in July 1919.

On the other hand, a doubt arises over the closeness of the relationship between he and Schwarz due to the fact Fair Play calls his subject Leslie Walter. The transposition of first names may have been an innocent mistake but it is unlikely in the case of people who knew one another well and were of similar ages. One thing is certain; someone on the *Chronicle* knew the identity of Fair Play. A final point in this argument: as a ranker with the Fusiliers, Schwarz's letters were censored. However, officers were allowed to censor their own mail.[12]

'Merritt' was also the name of the Toowoomba town clerk and the married name of Schwarz's older sister, Lily, who was a notable absentee from the Toowoomba civic reception that welcomed Schwarz home in 1922. Having a 'Merritt' back home meant Schwarz could have written to her under his assumed name without arousing suspicion. However, one look at his handwriting would have been enough to convince Lily that, far from being deserter, her younger brother had joined the British Army under his adopted name. We may speculate further that Schwarz in his 'plans already made' had conspired with his sister, before he left Australia, to use the name as his lifeline to his relatives. Schwarz never claimed that her married name, let alone that of the town clerk, influenced his decision to become Walter Merritt. Did he make the decision in England and, if so, who or what influenced his choice? Obviously, if my thesis is correct, a member or members of the brotherhood of Freemasons advised him on the choice of an alias. It must be considered a wise choice. It is a not atypical 'English' name judging by the fact there were at least four other Walter Merritts serving in the British forces in the First World War, more W. Merritts, even more Merritts with different first names and others with slight variations in the spelling of the surname.[13] We must accept Schwarz's decision to use his sister's married name was, therefore, no more than coincidence. Or was it?

Chapter 9

The King's Pardon

The effect of fuch pardon by the king, is to make the offender a new man; to acquit him of all corporal penalties and forfeitures annexed to that offence for which he obtains his pardon; and not fo much to reftore his former, as to give him a new, credit and capacity ... The king himfelf condemns no man; that rugged tafk he leaves to his courts of juftice: the great operation of his fceptre is mercy.

Blackstone's commentaries on the laws of England, Book the Fourth, chapter 31st of Reprieve and Pardon. Source: The Avalon Project at Yale Law School.

From this distance in time it is not possible to say how long the seriously wounded Schwarz lay on the battleground east of Ledgehem before he received medical help. It was his last day at war, 14 October 1918. Nor is it possible to know how many other wounded men around him were waiting in pain to be treated. Medical corpsmen were equipped with a field surgical haversack containing bandages, ¼-grain morphine tablets, scissors plaster and dressings. To ration the contents corpsmen would treat a wound, so long as it was not life threatening, using the field dressing each soldier carried in a waterproof pack in his jacket pocket. Ripping open its cover revealed a pad of gauze and an ampoule. Pressing it, the ampoule crumpled and released iodine over the pad, which the corpsman placed over the wound. We may assume the corpsman who attended Schwarz took one look at his shattered leg, flipped the cover of his haversack and proceeded to dress the wound in a more elaborate fashion. Before that he would have reached for the morphine tablets and, holding Schwarz's mouth open, placed them under his tongue. The corpsman would have seen a swift effect as the drug raced through Schwarz's bloodstream, colour returning to his face and warmth to his body.

Hours later, when Schwarz was admitted to a casualty clearing station (CCS), the frantically overworked doctors decided not to remove his leg, possibly in the hope it could be saved or because worse cases demanded their attention. Had they amputated, the leg would have been tossed into a basket. Once filled, orderlies carried the baskets to a tent where other baskets containing limbs stood in tidy rows awaiting disposal. Dr John Hayward, a British Army surgeon who later served in the Roehampton hospital where Schwarz was treated, was working in a CCS on the Western Front at the time Schwarz was wounded. It is possible he treated him – one of hundreds of cases. Hayward later wrote of the horrors he witnessed not for the sake of sensation, but to bring home the realities of war. It was impossible for him to convey the scene:

> Into the tent borne on stretchers or come wearily stumbling figures in khaki wrapped in blankets or coats, bandaged or splinted. All of them stiff with mud or caked with blood and dust and salt sweat … They come in such numbers that the tent is soon filled … Many are white and cold … The badly shocked had passed beyond it; others appeared numbed … here were lying uncomplaining men with shattered heads or ghastly disfiguration of their faces, others with shell and bullet wounds of the chest, spitting blood and gasping for breath … and here were 'multiple wounded' their bodies riddled with large and small shell fragments, terrible compound fractures … and the stumps of torn-off limbs.[1]

Schwarz was kept in the CCS for three days before he was considered stable enough to be moved. He was placed on a train with other wounded. At the end of the line ambulances were waiting to take them on the next part of their journey, to No. 5 Stationary Hospital, Wimereux. The author Evadne Price (under the pseudonym Helen Zenna Smith), based on her First World War experiences as an ambulance driver writes of collecting from railway station sidings 'trainloads of broken human beings: half-dead men pleading to be put out of their misery; torn and bleeding and crazed men … men with vacant eyes and mouths hanging foolishly apart dropping saliva and slime; men with minds mercifully gone; men only too sane, eyes horror-filled with blood and pain …' Her experiences haunted her. 'I fear these maimed men ... I am afraid they will stay with me all my life, shutting out beauty till the day I die ...'[2]

Schwarz's army records show he was admitted to No. 5 hospital on 17 October 1918 suffering 'gunshot wounds to the thigh and fractures'. He writes, 'my leg was found to be in such a state that to save my life it was amputated above the knee.' He remained a patient when hostilities ended on 11 November 1918, at the 11th hour.

As peace settled he received news that the king had approved the bar to his Military Cross. The citation published in the supplement to *The London Gazette* 30 July 1919, reads:

> T/2nd Lt Walter Lancelot Merritt, MC, R Fus Bde Intell Off HQ 86th Infy Bde. East of Ledgehem on October 14th, 1918, as brigade intelligence officer he carried the direction flag in the centre of the attack, and arrived on the first objective with only about forty men, the remainder having got lost in the thick fog and smoke. He and his observers captured twenty-eight Germans during the advance and they held the objective under heavy trench mortar and machine-gun fire until the remainder of the brigade arrived. He was severely wounded in the leg ... He behaved most gallantly and did fine work.

Schwarz tells us a message arrived in hospital from Brigadier General (Ronnie) Cheape that cheered him. It read:

> We are all so awfully sorry to hear that you have lost your leg, but cheer up it is far better to lose a leg than an arm. We got our objectives on the day you were wounded, as we always have in this Brigade, thanks to fellows like you.

For some time his survival was open to doubt. Nevertheless, Schwarz improved to the point where he was considered fit enough to travel. He left the hospital on 2 January 1919, crossed the Channel and was admitted to the 3rd London General Hospital, Wandsworth, for officer casualties. In this hospital Schwarz came close to having his cover blown. In February 1919 a fellow patient approached and greeted him in an Australian accent, 'Les Schwarz, I never thought we'd meet up like this.'

This was a man his own age whom he recognized: Ted Harders, a fellow cadet from the Toowoomba drill hall. An AIF lieutenant, he was wearing hospital issue pajamas under a dressing gown. He had been admitted suffering from the effects of mustard gas. Back home, he'd worked next door to the grocery store where Schwarz was employed as an assistant. The two had often lunched together. Despite the surprise, Schwarz stayed calm. He must have been mentally prepared for such a moment for years, knowing how much depended on his being able to bluff. 'You've mistaken me for someone else,' he snapped as he moved aside and limped away on his crutches, his heart pounding. Harders was sure the man he had confronted was his old friend. He asked a nursing sister had a man named Schwarz been admitted. She checked. No, the admission lists did not show a patient by that name.[3] Harders did not bother Schwarz again and a few days after the encounter Schwarz was transferred to the Special Orthopaedic Hospital at Southmead, Bristol, no doubt glad to be away from a man who could destroy his carefully contrived and maintained story. He had more operations at Southmead and after convalescing at Rock House, Bath, he was admitted to Dover House, Roehampton, to be fitted for an artificial limb. Further letters from comrades caught up with him here. One, dated 4 March 1919, was from Captain W. Dearden, Brigade Major, 86th Infantry Brigade Headquarters:

> I am most awfully sorry to hear that you have got such a rotten wound and have lost your leg. I hear that you did magnificently, and know you have the Military Cross and I don't know how many bars ... many, many congratulations, as you deserved all you got.

A second letter, dated 15 September 1919, was from the French interpreter attached to 86th Infantry Brigade HQ:

> I sincerely hope someone has kept a record of the speeches made at Christmas 1918, when from General Cheape to the French Froggy, best wishes were sent to two of the finest officers the British Army has had, Captain Dearden and Lieutenant Merritt. We missed you both very much, and I shall always look back to my stay with the staff of the 86th Infantry Brigade.

Schwarz was still a patient in April 1920 when a telegram boy arrived at Dover House. He handed Schwarz a flimsy envelope. It contained a handwritten message taken down by a telegraphist at the Bath post office:

Post Office Telegraphs [*sic*]
OHMS Buckingham Palace

[To] Lieut Walter Merritt
Dover House. Roehampton. Bath

Your attendance is required at Buckingham Palace on Thursday the twenty second inst at ten thirty o'clock am service dress please telegraph acknowledgment.

The king was to personally decorate him.

Schwarz was thrilled to acknowledge the telegram. He was not going to confess his deception before parading in full dress uniform before the king.

A half-hour before the ceremony was due to begin a taxi dropped Schwarz off in the palace forecourt. He limped through the main door between a guard of honour. Inside a flunkey told him to follow other recipients to the ballroom, where relatives of the heroes sat, awed by their surroundings, in their best dress. They surely brought for Schwarz the reality of his secret life and turned his mind to his loved ones thousands of miles away. He must have yearned for their presence in this, his proudest moment. His mother, after the ceremony, would have posed with him in the forecourt for a photograph as they had a decade earlier with Schwarz in his first uniform.

An attendant attached a small curtain hook to the left breast pocket of his uniform jacket and pointed to a row of chairs. Schwarz anxiously asked the man seated next to him a question he'd had on his mind since receiving the summons. Nobody at the hospital had had an answer: 'What is the procedure?'

'They told me I should watch and learn,' replied his fellow hero, who appeared equally as tense.

As His Majesty entered accompanied by palace staff, the recipients rose as one, though some, like Schwarz, did so with difficulty due to their wounds. George had spent the previous day at the races at Epsom and had done well in his betting.[4] During the war years he had become a dab hand at these ceremonies. There had been too many. The decorations were laid out on a table covered in a velvet cloth. Without preliminaries the ceremony began. The king's aide-de-camp read out the first citation, for a Scots Guards officer, who rose from his seat, marched to the king, stopped and saluted. The king shook his hand, spoke quiet words and then placed the medal on the hook dangling from his pocket. The Guardsman took two paces back, saluted again and resumed his seat. Schwarz had the 'procedure'. Eventually it was his turn to face the man to whom he had sworn allegiance, in his various roles, more often than any soldier in the First World War, possibly in any war. Had the king been alerted to Schwarz's background he would not have found himself shaking the man's hand, pinning a medal on his chest, asking after his health and telling him 'well done'. Schwarz, who had managed the required manoeuvre on his crutches, found the ceremony 'a very great honour'. He must have felt his Camelot idyll had come to life.

A week later, a letter arrived at the Queen Alexandra's Military Hospital, Millbank, London, where he was continuing his rehabilitation. It read:

The War Office,

Sir,

I am directed to inform you that the Medical Board by whom you were recently examined having expressed their opinion that you are permanently unfit for any future military service it is regretted that there is no alternative but to gazette you as relinquishing your commission on account of ill health caused by wounds, as from 5th May, 1920.

The requisite notification will appear in [*The London*] *Gazette* in due course when you will be permitted to retain the rank of lieutenant but such permission does not confer the right to wear uniform, except on appropriate occasions of a Military nature.

The case will be submitted to the Ministry of Pensions for their consideration as to any claim to retired pay or gratuity on account of disability. Payment is made monthly in arrears, and the Ministry of Pensions will endeavour to make the first payment, if any is due, one month after the date of relinquishment.

Schwarz received the news with 'the greatest regret'. It not only brought to an official end his ambition for a career as a permanent military officer, it also meant an organization outside the Army was about to open a file on him. Walter Lancelot Merritt did not exist except within British Army service records.

It was confession time.

His petition was sent to Buckingham Palace with the following covering letter:

Rokesley Lodge
95a St Georges Rd
Brighton
9th May 1921
To His Majesty the King

Your Majesty
I have endeavoured in the enclosed memorandum to tell my story in as few words as possible, and I humbly ask Your Majesty to read it, and if it should please Your Majesty I shall be very grateful if Your Majesty will grant me Your most gracious pardon, and also grant me permission to use the name under which I fought the Germans.

I have always served Your Majesty faithfully as a Private, and as an Officer. I honestly believe that I have carried out the terms of the Commission Your Majesty was pleased to grant me.

Although I have lost a limb I am still capable of bearing arms, and am quite prepared to lose all my limbs in Your service.

During the last National Emergency I offered my services to the War Office, and whenever Your Majesty calls for men I shall offer myself.

Hoping one day I shall again be allowed to serve Your Majesty.

I have the Honour to remain
Your Majesty's most humble servant
Walter L. Merritt
Lieutenant M.C.
(né Schwarz)

It was personally delivered to the king's private secretary, Colonel Clive Wigram. From his reaction we know Wigram was initially humanely stirred by the unique nature of Schwarz's appeal. Further we may assume he saw potential embarrassment to the king in the petition's revelation that Schwarz had been a guest at Buckingham Palace under his alias where he 'had the very great honour of receiving my Military Cross and Bar from the hands of His Majesty.' The king had also approved his commission under false circumstances – he had given de facto approval to Schwarz as Merritt. The man had fooled him. Wigram considered it was a matter that needed to be settled discreetly. But how?

Had Schwarz pleaded for a pardon for desertion and any other sins the powers that be may consider he had committed, Wigram may have immediately brought Australian officials into the matter. However, his plea was equally for permissions to continue to use his alias 'Walter Lancelot Merritt'. So instead Wigram turned to the War Office for advice. On 12 May 1921 he wrote to Sir Herbert Creedy, a career civil servant then aged forty-two who had joined the War Office as a clerk in 1901 and risen steadily through its ranks.

> I think I had better send on to you this petition … It is a pathetic story, and if … correct, he seems to have made good.
>
> At the same time he is probably anxious lest he should be arrested and sent back to Australia for trial. Perhaps you could let me know whether anything can be done to assist his wishes, or advise me as to the answer I should send.

Wigram's note contains the assumption that Schwarz's claims will need to be confirmed. A month after his first letter to the WO, Wigram wrote again asking for more information about Schwarz. Once again he was left unenlightened. Objectively Schwarz's plea had the potential to embarrass the War Office as well as the palace should his story become public. Here was a young man from the 'colonies' who had fooled the British Army for years with apparent immunity while turning himself into a hero, accepted for all intents and purposes as a fine example of a gallant son of an Englishman, a born to lead officer, a man physically well-built, handsome in appearance, in short, the best of Anglo-Saxon stock. Whereas he was, more so than the king, of German stock. The blood of England's enemies ran through his veins.

When Creedy did eventually respond to Wigram, on 26 May 1921, it was to tell him he'd come up with an idea. As Schwarz had 'deserted from an Australian regiment I am consulting the authorities at Australia House [in London] on the question of a grant of a pardon to him …' This was the first time the pardon and desertion became the purpose of the petition. The two were thus inexorably joined in history. Creedy asked the Australia House Official Secretary, M.J. Shepherd, 'If your military advisers think this is a case for the exercise of clemency … you will let me know, we can take the necessary formalities in hand.'

It was an ultimatum. Shepherd was not given anything more than the petition to go on and was not told whether the WO had sought to verify Schwarz's claims of his life as Merritt. All the WO boffin was asking the Australians to do was show compassion, make the grand gesture and trust them. By implication any other transgressions that may have concerned Schwarz-Merritt were to be overlooked by an equal gesture from the king and his advisers. To help them along, Creedy portentously added: 'If his desertion had been from a British regiment, I think it is almost certain that we should have recommended His Majesty to grant him a free pardon. It's a fact that Merritt was twice mentioned in dispatches (MiD) and was awarded the Military Cross and Bar in the circumstances set out by him.' The comment ignores the reality of the British treatment of deserters. As discussed in earlier chapters, hundreds of British deserters – including officers – were executed for the crime. Excuses more plausible than that offered by Schwarz were ignored.

Australia House gave Creedy's refrain a sympathetic reception. 'I think that in view of the war services rendered by Schwarz, steps might be taken to recommend his pardon for desertion,' came the 4 June reply, under the signature of Shepherd. However, he added, it would be necessary to refer the matter to Australian Prime Minister Billy Hughes, who was at that time in London. The PM was on a busy schedule and passed it on to his defence minister, Pearce, back in Australia. The petition with its charges of discrimination represented further grounds for embarrassment in this case for Australia's military forces. Yet it appears Pearce did not order any further inquiry into its contents. We do not know what action he took beyond the cursory before telling Australia House to let the War Office know he agreed with and approved its view that the case was one for clemency, adding it (the WO) was the proper authority to take the necessary formalities to resolve the matter. We may assume Pearce looked on Schwarz's petition with innate sympathy. He was the fifth of eleven children of English parents. He was born and grew up in the Adelaide Hills town of Mount Barker, South Australia, where his father worked as a blacksmith. The area had a strong German community. Many of its families had been settled there for three, even four generations and counted themselves as more Australian than the recently arrived Pearces.

The defence minister had opposed the early restriction on men with German names joining the AIF. On his watch thousands of men of German origin had died or been wounded fighting for the British, including men from the Hills communities. Pearce overruled considerable opposition to the appointment of the son of Prussian parents, General John Monash, to lead the Australia forces in Europe. Schwarz's service as conscientious army cadet in the compulsory military training scheme was another plus for Pearce, who had implemented and extended the scheme before the war. As we have seen, the majority of the electorate was opposed to the training of senior cadets, that is, boys aged thirteen to eighteen. Attendance at parades was poor; many who did show up lacked discipline. The Schwarz family was an exception. Pearce was a pro-conscriptionist, another stance that left him open to public criticism. Schwarz had not waited to be conscripted. He had in his unique way proved the benefit of Pearce's unpopular scheme.

By now Schwarz's story had reached the attention of Sir Laming Worthington-Evans, who months before had replaced Winston Churchill as Secretary of State for War. He took a personal interest in the matter. Sir Laming ordered the drawing up of a formal petition that he personally signed and addressed in scroll writing thus:

Most humbly submitted to Your Majesty by Your Majesty's Most Humble and Most Devoted Servant.

It reads:

The petition of Temporary Lieutenant Walter L. Merritt MC, late Royal Fusiliers, for a pardon in respect of his desertion in October 1915, from the Australian Expeditionary [sic] Force, in which he served in the ranks under his true name of Schwarz.

... It is recommended that Your Majesty may be graciously pleased to approve the grant of a pardon in view of the exceptional gallantry in action displayed by the Petitioner subsequent to this offence.

The memorandum accompanying the submission sets out the detail Schwarz gave in his petition. It adds that the Army Council approves the pardon.

The king scratched with an ink pen on the scroll: 'Appd G.R.V.' The king had approved. The end of the matter. Schwarz's story had passed with little or no scrutiny, his pardon for desertion transmuting into a parallel pardon for his subterfuges in joining the Fusiliers and gaining a king's commission.

Schwarz was told of his pardon in a letter dated 31 July signed by Colonel Clive Wigram. Subsequently he wrote to the War Office asking it to repatriate him saying he could not have applied beforehand as he had been ranked as a deserter. The WO obliged him on this matter, one suspects not so much out of a spirit of generosity as by the desire to see the last of the hero who had become an inconvenience.

Schwarz's request in his petition to continue using the name 'under which I fought the Germans' could well indicate a desire to settle in Britain. Also, he may have feared his original name would lead to discrimination in a post-war climate. A further reason, he had become comfortable in the role of a decorated English officer. However, the world was moving on. In his letter advising Schwarz of his pardon Creedy tells him to apply to the Home Office for permission to retain his alias. A separate letter from Creedy dated 8 August 1921 to Shepherd at Australia House makes it clear under what name the king's pardon was granted – Schwarz. The Home Office did not oblige Schwarz. Walter Lancelot Merritt had breathed his last.

As he healed physically and mentally a desire he had long suppressed surfaced and began to dominate his thoughts: a longing to see his mother, brother, sisters and friends again after years of subterfuge, of the horrors of war, of long-term pain and suffering. As Walter Leslie Schwarz he could fulfil this longing, what's more, return home without fear of prosecution, a hero under his real name.

Postscript

Comparisons are, as they say, odious. However, it does serve a purpose to mention here the story of an AIF deserter whose true identity, among his other deceptions, remained unquestioned for most of his long life mainly it appears because, as with the Schwarz mystery, nobody bothered to examine or inquire into the truth or otherwise. The man's word was accepted by a bureaucracy whose officials never asked Harold Katte, who changed his name to Marcel Caux, about his claims and his dodgy actions. As a consequence nearly a century later he embarrassed Australia's military establishment when it agreed to portray Caux's image on a prize-winning design for a recruiting poster. His first deception came in September 1915, when Katte enlisted. As Schwarz did with the Fusiliers, he lied about his age, swearing he was eighteen, when he was sixteen. A member of the AIF 2nd Division, he was wounded three times, including in 1916 at Pozières and in 1918 near Villers-Bretonneux in the battle of Amiens when a bullet shattered his knee, ending his war. Katte's worst lies came after the war when he rewrote his life under the name Marcel Caux. He claimed to have been born in France. Katte was born 1 March 1899 in the inner-Sydney working-class suburb of Marrickville. In addition to the poster, the Australian Government in 2004 gave him a state funeral under his false name. Before his death the French Government decorated him with the Legion of Honour. Following the funeral *Sydney Morning Herald* journalist Tony Stephens revealed Katte was not the hero of poster fame. Katte had twice deserted his comrades in France. His first absence lasted a week in July 1917, for which he served fourteen days in close confinement. In June the following year, French authorities arrested him in the port of Brest, where he was said to be posing as a Frenchman. An Australian court martial jailed him for ten days. When historian and author Lynette Silver discovered there was no record of a Caux in Australia's First World War forces,[5] the Department of Veterans' Affairs explained away its failure to verify his various claims and entitlements by saying he had wished to retain some anonymity. He had good reason. He married Irma Davis in 1929. Although there is no record of a divorce, he married Doris Young in 1949, claiming he was born in Quebec. Silver points out that he had five names, five signatures, three nationalities, three places of birth, three dates of birth, three mothers, three fathers and two wives, simultaneously. Katte's story shows that, on balance, Schwarz, despite some pause, made the correct decision to confess whether on his own initiative or guided by those who, I argue, had helped him during his Merritt years. Lies and aliases may be acceptable in war but, come the peace, they will follow you to your grave – and beyond.

Chapter 10

'There is No Doubt that my Father was of German Extraction'

Schwarz lied and was almost certainly guilty of conspiring with others to attain his goals. The most benign view we may take of this is that his bravery in the end spoke louder than his misdeeds. Should we accept this as the reason for his actions, it becomes possible not to make moral judgments to, indeed, let the untruths die with the passing of time so that the heroic legend remains. That would leave us with a false history.

Until Schwarz walked out of the 55th Battery Siege Brigade base near Lydd, Kent, on the morning of Saturday, 23 October 1915, we have no reason to believe he was anything but an honest and upright young man of simple tastes, albeit with a singular ambition, thwarted by circumstances beyond his control, a career in the Army as a commissioned officer. However, his desertion was not a spontaneous gesture. It was based on 'plans already made'. This cryptic phrase leads us to the belief he was not alone in his actions. It is also a claim that it appears he was never, in all the scrutiny his petition came under, called upon to explain. Or if he had, to whomever or whenever, his explanation remains a secret to this day. For example, Schwarz says, as we have seen, 'I was taken off the battery commander's staff [Hurst's], and detailed for duty as a mess orderly.' But when he confronts his commanding officer, Coxen tells him to 'see my battery commander [Hurst].' Several interpretations of these passages suggest themselves:

1. Coxen had been unaware of the dismissal;
2. Schwarz, for some reason, chose not to point out to Coxen that Hurst was no longer his battery commander, that he came under command of whoever was in charge of the mess;

3. Schwarz's removal from the battery was temporary;
4. He lied in his petition in that he was still on Hurst's staff at the time he had deserted.

The above suggests the petition, which passed through many hands from the king down, did so without seemingly anyone subjecting it to the kind of scrutiny such an extraordinary document surely deserved and needed.

On the Saturday Schwarz walked out of the siege brigade camp he did not apply for a weekend or day pass to travel to London. It was either a brazen gesture, or he was confident that he was safe in London, unconcerned that diligent provosts who patrolled the streets and places where soldiers hung out may ask him to show his permission to be abroad. Schwarz booked a bed at the Union Jack Club in Sandell Street, opposite Waterloo Station. I contend he never intended to stay there; it was a ruse. Nor did he intend to spend time on the streets in uniform.

In dealing with the mystery of Schwarz's whereabouts in London that weekend I start with the assumption he stayed at 23 Warrender Road, Holborn, in the Islington Borough. It was the address he gave the Fusiliers' recruiting officers the following Monday as his current residence. In 1915, many Anzacs had relatives in Britain and one in four AIF recruits was British-born.[1] On leave, their relatives welcomed them into their homes. Schwarz's nearest kin were closer to Berlin than London. So who welcomed him at the front door of 23?

Warrender Road snakes through London's smallest and one of its oldest boroughs. It covers an area of just over 6 square miles. It boasts some of the most famous Georgian squares in London, a canal system and the Arsenal Football Club. Today, as with inner suburban areas in other large cities, new residents have refurbished its houses and made it a vibrant community.[2] The picture was different early last century. Islington was a slum, possibly the worst in London, a home to the poorer working-class families living in rundown tenements; families shared houses with one, sometimes two other families. Overcrowding was 'terrible with a family's beds jam-packed into the same room; humping water up the stairs from a standpipe in the back yard for cooking or washing and sharing an outside toilet with several other families.[3] Number 23, at the north end of the road, near High Holborn, was little different to its rundown neighbours. Schwarz could not have claimed a more miserable place to call home.

Apart from the notation on his recruitment papers, the address does not appear in Schwarz's story, until now. At first glance the address could be taken as Schwarz, or somebody on his behalf, having a lend of officialdom when filling out the recruitment forms in that the first three letters of the name are WAR and 23 is the date he deserted the AIF. In other words, was it a randomly chosen but necessary detail for the form? It was and is to this day a genuine house address.

The house and its inhabitants are an intriguing part of this story. As we have seen, the war had brought workers from all parts of the country to London, making housing conditions more crowded and hard to find. From what we now know it is not surprising to find the names of Schwarz or Merritt were not on the electoral registrar in 1915. It is a surprise to find that, given the demand for accommodation, the electoral role shows one person was in this period the registered occupant of 23, a Charles Edwin Croucher. Other occupants there may have been, possibly a wife or female companion, children and other relatives. Women did not appear on the electoral register until the UK Parliament gave them the vote. It did so in 1918, and then to females aged thirty or more. The one thing we are able to assume from Croucher's listing is that no more than one adult male lived there officially at a time when Schwarz gave it as his address. Had Croucher been the sole resident of 23, then we are able to assume it was no longer a home for a family or families.

If Schwarz had registered with the Sportsman's Battalion before deserting – 'plans already made' – he needed an address at which to receive call-up papers, a safe house where no questions were asked, one that provided accommodation and a valid address. If 23 were such a place, how did he find it, or who directed him to it? As we have seen, he did not have relatives in London, not in Warrender Road, or elsewhere. A civilian address in London would have been useful for Schwarz – and others – for many reasons, one of them, an unofficial postal address for collecting and sending letters, especially for soldiers who wanted to avoid the eyes of the military censors. Croucher had left the house by 1919 and new tenants moved in the following year.

However and wherever Schwarz spent the weekend, come Monday morning when he appeared at the Fusiliers' recruiting depot in Scotland Yard he could not be wearing or carrying anything that would identify him as an AIF soldier. Beforehand he had to dispose of his army issue underwear, slouch hat, greatcoat, jacket, trousers, puttees, boots, identification discs, pay book and personal papers such as letters. Nothing must be found on him that would reveal either his true name or his service with the AIF. Once again, 23 Warrender Road suggests itself as a convenient place to shed the old uniform, no questions asked. Physically he had nothing to give himself away. Unlike some of his comrades, he had not had himself tattooed. Except for vaccination marks and the scar on his small right-hand finger, his body was unmarked.

As he puts it, a part of his weekend was spent acquiring civilian clothes. This would have presented as a major problem had he done so in AIF uniform and until he had made the acquisition he had no other clothes. Had he shopped in a gentlemen's tailors or similar conventional establishment, customers and shop assistants would obviously have suspected the Digger was up to no good. Schwarz's knowledge of the Army Act would have made him aware that anyone, it did not have to be the military police, could arrest a man without a warrant based upon a reasonable suspicion he may be a deserter or an absentee without leave. Should a shop's owner sell clothes to such a man, police could charge him with aiding and abetting a criminal. Others had to have bought the clothes for him.

A court martial found the first British soldier executed in the war for desertion guilty on the grounds he was in civilian clothes at the time of his arrest. He was Private Thomas Highgate, No. 10061, of the 1st Battalion, Royal West Kent Regiment. Born in Gravesend, a farm labourer, he was months short of his eighteenth birthday when he enlisted on 4 February 1913. Schwarz too had signed on before the war. Both men were unmarried. Military police found Highgate in a barn in France. He told them he could not remember anything from the time he had left his bivouac earlier that day. His offence, trial and the confirmation of the death sentence took place on the same day – 6 September 1914. Unlike Schwarz, Highgate had kept his army identity papers and pay book and stated his regimental affiliation. At no time did he deny he was a British soldier as Schwarz was to deny he was an Australian soldier. The British Army *Manual of Military Law* (1914), Chapter 3, section 13, states:

> The offence of desertion – that is to say, of deserting or attempting to desert His Majesty's service – implies an intention on the part of the offender either not to return to His Majesty's service at all, or to escape some particular important service.

The AIF law was based on the British law that provided a soldier illegally wearing civilian clothes meant he had absented himself in a deliberate or clandestine manner. It had nothing to do with how far he was from his camp or barracks. A court martial was entitled to assume he was a deserter, liable to be shot. Under this law, Schwarz would not have stood a chance of acquittal by a court martial. In any case, he was found guilty in absentia.

In Highgate's case, the arresting officer, a Captain C.A. Milward, did not reveal anything about the teenager's motives or offer a specific reason why the soldier had shed his uniform. The officers sitting in judgement were apparently disinterested in a deserter's mental or physical condition. Nobody gave evidence to show Highgate had not been a bad soldier; an officer from his battalion did not give evidence as to his disciplinary record, character and soldierly qualities. Orders came from the top; a firing squad was to execute Highgate at once and as publicly as possible – the intention being to deter others. The execution took place in front of men from 15 Brigade. His fate was circulated to the rest of the Army. In the First World War, firing squads executed more than 300 British soldiers.[4] As losses mounted in AIF ranks, a number of its officers lobbied for Australia to introduce the death sentence for desertion. It was not. One reason for this apparently humane, not to say enlightened, policy, it is argued, was the reaction in Australia to the execution of two of its soldiers, Breaker Morant and P.J. Handcock, in the Boer War by orders of the British, for the murder of prisoners and a German missionary.

At the Royal Fusiliers depot on the Monday morning, Schwarz told the duty officer, a Captain Rickards, his name was Walter Lancelot

Merritt and that he was the son of Henry (Merritt), an Englishman who had migrated to Australia and married. In his petition to King George V, Schwarz, contradicts this claim, writing that both his parents were born in Australia and 'there is no doubt that my father was of German extraction.' Strictly speaking, as we have seen, his father, Heinrich, was born at sea on an Australia-bound voyage. Apart from being the truth it was a subtle invocation to the Germanic blood coursing through the veins of the king and his queen. Schwarz also claimed he and his father worked as office clerks. His father was a labourer and after leaving school Schwarz had worked as a grocer's assistant. These inconsistencies in Schwarz's personal account may be put down to the desire of the young man to show himself in the best possible light. However, they also draw attention to flaws in his story that have been difficult to check after the passage of almost a century from the momentous events through which the story flows.

The battalion medical officer who examined Schwarz was a retired fleet surgeon whose signature is illegible on Schwarz's records. In response to this officer's questions, Schwarz said he was born in 'Melbourne Parish County Australia'. The address is a nonsense. Melbourne is the capital of the State of Victoria, a major city as it was then and is today, much more than a parish. The surgeon may be forgiven for his geographical ignorance in overlooking this. But not for the other part of the address that appears on the official form: Australia is and was more than a county (of Britain). ... Maybe the MO could not have been bothered with such detail. If so it was a reflection of his contempt for this young recruit – and by inference for others who came before him in the process of putting their lives on the line for king and country. However, what I regard as the most probable reason, he was aware the truth was not a criterion in dealing with a man who was not what he claimed to be. In fact, Schwarz was born more than a thousand miles (1,600km) from 'Parish Melbourne', in Toowoomba, Queensland.

The fleet surgeon did note accurately the physical details, which appearance alone meant they could not be so carelessly disputed: 5 feet 11 inches (180cm) tall, some inches taller than the average Tommy. Chest expansion 37 inches (93cm), weight 156 pounds (72kg approximately). Schwarz deposed he was aged twenty-one years. He was nineteen.

Also noted were four vaccination marks on his left arm. These were for smallpox and enteric fever. He missed the scar on the small finger of Schwarz's right hand. Despite these lapses, the doctor was satisfied as to Schwarz's state of health, marking it down as excellent and further noting Schwarz gave his religion as 'C of E' (Church of England) and his next of kin as Nellie Merritt of James Street, Toowoomba, Queensland. Another false notation. James Street is the longest street in Toowoomba, passing through the town east to west. At either end, it becomes the main highway to and from Brisbane and western Queensland. In his AIF attestation, papers for service abroad that he had filled out three months earlier, Schwarz had responded truthfully to the question 'Who is your next of kin? (Address to be stated)' with 'Mrs Augusta Schwarz, Eleanor St, Toowoomba'. Joyce Hampson, a cousin, recalled some years later in a *Toowoomba Chronicle* article that Schwarz had lived here with his mother and a sister. Accompanying the article is a photo of the double-fronted cottage with its bull-nosed verandah and white picket fence. Its appearance is still recognizable from that description today. To her family and friends Mrs Schwarz (née Otto) was known as Minnie, not Nellie.

While on the subject of his assumed names, I should make it clear I am aware citizens may change their own name – if not others – so long as they do not do it to deceive. Schwarz's intent was deception.

The origin of his new middle name with its Arthurian connotations remains unexplained. Lancelot was not in common usage then or now. Schwarz may have hoped it would stress the claim to his English inheritance. However, why would Schwarz take the risk of choosing an unusual name when a common one, for example, John, Peter or Nigel, would have served his purpose? Neither Rickards, Jordan nor the medical officer asked Schwarz to produce means of identification. He had none.

A major lie was, of course, his denial he had served in another branch of His Majesty's forces. Months before he had sworn to 'truly serve our Sovereign Lord the King in the Australian Imperial Forces', the AIF then being a semi-autonomous branch of His Majesty's forces. His claim to being a 'raw' recruit was sufficient to have had him charged with fraudulent enlistment, a crime punishable by imprisonment. Had he admitted to previous service the recruit officers would have asked for details, a discharge certificate and character references. Once again, Schwarz had none.

Rickards attested he had taken care the recruit understood each question that had been put to him and that his enlistment papers were correct and properly filled out. Had a senior officer, or any other responsible person, bothered to confirm the basic facts, such as the London address Schwarz gave – a street not a few miles from the depot – found Schwarz had lied and initiated an investigation, Schwarz's life would have unravelled and Rickards (and Jordan) could have been prosecuted under military law for aiding and abetting a false induction, whether they had acted consciously or not. When, years later, Schwarz confessed all, the enlistment details were not altered. They reside in the files of British Army records as 'Merritt' had given them to this day.

Australia had introduced compulsory military training for males beginning once a boy had turned twelve. It had given Schwarz his first taste of military life at an early age. Aged eighteen, he left the Cadet Corps for the Regular Army, going from a cadet corps officer to private, but with the resolve that one day he would again be an officer. Had he not enlisted he would have had to continue part-time service in the militia. Assuming Rickards did believe Schwarz's responses to the enlistment questions were genuine, we may put down to his ignorance of Australia's compulsory service his failure to query Schwarz's response to the question relating to prior service. Had Rickards done so, Schwarz would have had to explain why for the past nine years he had dodged his duty.

In July 1915, the British Government had set up a compulsory national register of persons between the ages of fifteen and sixty-five. Its intention was to ensure that people in this age bracket should play a role in the war effort that best suited their abilities.[5] It is hardly likely that Schwarz, who had arrived in England in June with the AIF, managed to register under his alias. Yet he was not asked why he had not done so.[6]

Schwarz allows us to believe his exit from the 55th Artillery Brigade was a spontaneous gesture as a result of the negative responses from his superior officers to his questions that Saturday morning on whether he would be sent into the fighting. Rather – and this is an insight into his cryptic 'plans already made' – he must have registered for military duty with the Sportsman's unit under his alias at an earlier date to have received a notice that would have given him the date and time he was to report at the Fusiliers depot for the enlistment process, i.e. 25 October. That is, the day he deserted the AIF. An army form Schwarz filled in on 3 December 1916 reveals a possible clue for his first contact with the Sportsman's.[7] Under the heading 'date of enlistment', he wrote '1-10-1915', a Friday, three weeks before he walked into the depot at Scotland Yard. A mistake on his part? One way or the other, yes.

Regarding the above, in drawing up his royal petition Schwarz mentions he researched dates relating to personal events in his army career. Research for this book shows some of the dates he gives are not accurate when compared to his official service record. The above date was either one of them, further proof of his pre-desertion plans or a mistake, the latter possibly due to the fact that by December 1916 he'd served time in the trenches under fire, had been wounded and was shell-shocked. Whatever reason, it also stands in the British files as an accurate record. Schwarz responded 'yes' to the question had he received his notice, saying a J. Henderson of the Royal Fusiliers had given it to him. He was not asked when and where Henderson had done so.

Having one way or another completed the enrolment process, Schwarz says from the depot he was posted to the 1st Sportsman's Battalion, 23rd Royal Fusiliers Battalion at Gidea Park, Romford.

In fact, he went to the newly formed 30th Sportsman's Reserve Battalion, RF. It owed its creation in part to the fact that the first two battalions were over-strength as a result of the number of applicants. The 30th was originally to have become the 3rd Sportsman's Battalion. It would provide replacements for the other two battalions. Office clerks recorded his arrival the following day. We may assume he was one of a number signed in. Neither recruiting officers nor training officers allow recruits to arrive singly or as and when they please. The Sportsman's Battalion officers allowed Schwarz to step smoothly into his assumed persona.

As a part-time cadet corps officer, Schwarz had demonstrated an ability to attract patrons; senior officers took the fatherless teenager under their wings and spent time encouraging him in his ambition for a military career. When he deserted, we must assume he once again put himself in the hands of people who helped him to further that career. Unlike the cadet officers, his later helpers risked criminal charges for aiding a deserter. For a reason I will come to, they may have considered the risk to be low. Furthermore, his helpers may have taken comfort from the fact that what Schwarz wanted from them was likely to result in his death before disclosure.

Schwarz's confidence that he was succeeding under his new identity may be illustrated in his claim that taking part, in November 1915, in a drill and bayonet fighting course with the Fusiliers he boasted, 'I obtained the highest number of marks in my class and was awarded a good certificate.' Had he been less secure, a man in his position, who had sworn he had no previous military training, should have pretended he was actually learning something. His failure to do so, in fact, to excel at other tasks of which he supposedly had no knowledge, raises further suspicions that his background was known in certain quarters and discretion took the form of an unspoken alliance. In other words, Schwarz was secure in his new role. A further pointer towards collusion is seen in the fact Schwarz had no trouble persuading the 30th Reserve Battalion commanding officer, Colonel H.J.H. Inglis, to send him, a shell-shocked invalid, back to war, where he wanted to be. He tells us in another cryptic allusion that his 'persuasion' amounted to him again resorting 'to my old tactics'. He does not expand on this comment.

Schwarz says his commanding officer in November 1916, Colonel Vernon DSO, recommended him for a commission. However, he had made an unsolicited application for promotion to officer rank in July 1916. It had lapsed when he returned to France. That application came with necessary references from persons of standing in the community who attested they personally knew him (Merritt, that is) and had done so for years. A Councillor Peter Campbell Cairns of the City of Glasgow Corporation, of 39 Whitfield Road, Ibrox, Glasgow, certified to the good moral character of Walter Lancelot Merritt for the past four years. Councillor Cairns represented the 27th Ward of the council from 1914 to 1920, when he retired. In 1914, the council had granted him leave of absence for one year to go on active service, one year we may reliably say in which his path did not cross Merritt's, who, in any case, had not existed four years earlier. Campbell died on 29 July 1944. *The Glasgow Herald* noted:

> The death occurred on Saturday in a hospital of Mr Peter Campbell Cairns, 75 Jamaica Street, Glasgow, a former member of Glasgow Town Council. Before the redistribution of wards after the last war, Mr Cairns represented the former Plantation Ward. For many years he served as a chief cook with Allan Line, and for some time he was secretary of a trade union connected with the shipping industry.[8]

A virtuous life. The story does not say with what branch of the military he served. We may assume, given his occupation, it was the Royal Navy.

A further reference came from a Philip Henderson, headmaster of Yardheads Public School, Leith, who certified in both applications that 'from personal knowledge ... Corporal W.L. Merritt has attained a standard of education suitable for commissioned rank.' This personal reference was vital as Schwarz was naturally unable to provide the necessary alternative proof that he had reached the education standard necessary for entry into the Royal Military College or Officer Training Courses (OTC). It was required, in time of war and peace, that a candidate should produce one of the following: a British school leaving or qualifying certificate; army entrance examination certificate; or a university entrance form. These were all reasonable basic qualifications for men who would be leaders. My attempts to find out more about Headmaster Henderson were unsuccessful. One reason I wanted to know was, what was his relationship to the J. Henderson of the Fusiliers who had handed Schwarz his call-up papers? It goes without saying the headmaster's testimony was wrong. We do know Schwarz had left school early to help support his family but, as we have seen, there is confusion to this day where he received his less than adequate education. Schwarz could not have produced an Australian equivalent of any of the above and that is an obvious reason why he failed to qualify for entry into Australia's Royal Military College, Duntroon, rather than his claimed lack of means.

On his first application for the OTC Schwarz wrote, in one response to item 13 (Schools or Colleges at which educated), 'South. Boys. School.

Twmba [*sic*]'. Schwarz must have calculated the Army would not contact the school in faraway Queensland. Had it done so, the school could not have provided a record of a former student named Walter Merritt, with all the implications that implied. The South Toowoomba State School opened in 1865 and split into boys and girls schools in 1869. Both were primary schools; neither could have given Schwarz the higher education that would have qualified a cadet applicant to proceed to an OTC. He had only Henderson's attestation to overcome this obstacle to his career path.

In his second application for a commission, he filled out a slightly different form in which item 13 does not appear on the printed section. However, at the bottom of the page is written in ink '12A School or Schools', at which the rest of the item and any other writing that followed has been removed, either by a tear or fraying. The damage extends into the next page, finishing just below Henderson's attestation that he found Schwarz to be educationally qualified. We are left with questions and conjectures. Why was the item written in when this second official form for OTC candidates did not provide for it? Had Schwarz once again named the primary school as his only place of education and someone decided any queries made on that detail would cause trouble for all concerned in the application?

Alternatively, Schwarz may not have met either Cairns or Henderson. They may have gone to their grave unaware their names and reputations had been commandeered to help Schwarz achieve the position in society he had long aspired to: an officer and a gentleman. Less kindly we take it they had been fully aware of their actions and acted under an obligation we deal with in the next chapter.

In his application Schwarz signed over the line denoted for Usual Signature of Candidate, 'W. Lancelot Merritt'.[9] His signature until now had been Walter Lancelot Merritt. However, by this stage, it appears he could have signed himself King George without raising a query. Colonel Inglis accepted the application on 5 August and certified he could recommend Schwarz 'as a suitable candidate in every way for admission to an Officer Cadet Unit with a view to being appointed to a commission'.

Some would say it was commendable in time of war that red tape was a necessary casualty. However, it begs the question, how many records on the files of British war archives are tainted as much as those of Schwarz/Merritt?

Vernon did not so much recommend as rubber stamp Schwarz's second application, which he made on 4 November 1916. For this attempt, Schwarz had found a new character referee, a Captain Rattray, of Edinburgh, who certifies – as Councillor Cairns and Headmaster Henderson had both done in Schwarz's original application – that he had known Schwarz (i.e. Merritt) for the previous four years and found him to be of good moral character. Four years earlier, Schwarz had been a part-time soldier and grocer's assistant in Toowoomba. It is not beyond the bounds of possibility that Captain Rattray happened to be in the Queensland town at the time and had since kept in touch – but it is unlikely. The application form provides that if a referee could not 'certify for the whole period of four years, a second certificate for the period not covered by the first should be signed by a person …who has been well acquainted with the candidate in private life during the period'. The space for a second certificate is empty.

Schwarz's claim that his satisfactory work had prompted Vernon to recommend him rings false. He had been on a personal campaign for promotion since that first application in July. Finally, he found an officer, Vernon, who accommodated him.

In both applications, Schwarz had written his birth date as 17 April 1894, two years earlier than the date on his birth certificate. This overcame the necessity of him being treated as a minor, therefore needing a parent or guardian to sign the OTC application. This was another awkward problem overcome and accepted by authority.

Once again, Schwarz in his petition lets the king know he was a high achiever. 'At a final interview, Colonel Williams [the cadet battalion commanding officer] informed me that I had done well in my examinations and that he had no hesitation in recommending me for a commission.' The young grocer's assistant from Toowoomba had bypassed the need for educational qualifications and genuine character references to 'return' to officer rank.

The supplement to *The London Gazette* 16 May 1917 lists Merritt among those newly appointed to temporary officer rank. A year after making his first application, Schwarz applied to have the commission made permanent, stating he intended to continue his military career post-war. Obviously to do so he would have had to live in Britain under the name Merritt. Had he accepted a British war pension as Merritt he would have spent the rest of his life in fear of exposure – for a start, taking money under false pretences. However, as a deserter, he had foregone his rights to an Australian war pension and other benefits extended to its ex-servicemen. Maintaining his alias in civilian life was going to be complicated. As Merritt he was entitled to apply for post-war education under the Officers University and Technical Classes Scheme. Should he do so, would the educational standard the Leith headmaster swore Schwarz had attained in his application for a commission stand up to examination? Would it put the reputation of Headmaster Henderson and Schwarz, on the line?

Once he attempted to make his way in civilian life as Merritt he would have to do so without points of reference. It had been all very well for the Army to accept him for who he had said he was while turning a blind or colluding eye to the less than remote possibility he was not. Civilian life was not going to treat him so kindly. It was a time for the truth to come out, or at least that much of the truth that would save him from prosecution.

It is almost certain that Schwarz in considering his future and what steps he should take to exonerate himself found trusty helpers from the same source as those who had brought him this far in his extraordinary career. One report says he approached Brigadier General (Ronnie) Cheape, his last commanding officer, and revealed his true identity.[10] The implication here is that Cheape advised him to confess.

Schwarz allowed the petition to the king to be looked upon as his own work. However, it is obvious that at least one other person was involved, a professional typist. But a thorough examination of the petition leads one to the inevitable conclusion that he was advised and guided on its content, that is, another person or persons helped him compile the petition before it was sent to Buckingham Palace. For example, he claims in the petition his parents were born in Australia when in fact his father was born at sea. Why lie about what at first glance appears to be a trivial matter? It was possibly pointed out to him that the convention is, as a sea birth baby, Heinrich's father would have taken on the nationality of his parents – German. His advisors may well have told him this could be a problem. The king may well have been reluctant to pardon the son of a German-born man at this time.

In his memorandum to His Majesty recommending a pardon for Schwarz, Secretary of State for War Sir Laming Worthington-Evans appears to have thought this matter of birth was worth making. He cites it not as a fact but as Schwarz's claim in his petition. He had to be cautious because obviously nobody had attempted to verify the claim, or to check other facts. We have seen how he had incorrectly stated a number of dates, such as the arrival of the 55th Siege Artillery Brigade in England. The misspelling of his AIF battery commander's name, 'Coxon' for 'Coxen' in the petition is further proof of others' involvement. This last error may have been the fault of a person who did not have access to the AIF officers' list. Even so, Schwarz would not have made the spelling mistakes had the petition been all his own work.

The petition's text shows a standard of English more than could be expected from a man who left school at primary level. Contrast it with the letter he wrote to his mother that she sent on to the Defence Department. A random example from the petition: we see in correct grammatical context 'commanders' assistants' and a few lines later, 'commander's staff'. Specifically, as we have seen, he uses two circumlocutions, i.e. 'plans already made', and 'resorted to my old tactics' to avoid revealing facts that may be self-incriminating or disclose the identities of those who had helped him and were privy to his secrets. The conclusion: others aided Schwarz in creating the petition. They not only had a better education but knew the protocols involved in a formal address to the king. These persons were obviously of some importance.

We may assume the helpers were in touch with the palace before submitting it. They would have been aware a document of this sensitivity and rarity could not be allowed to arrive unannounced in the post. The person on the staff who first set eyes on it had to be someone who realized its significance and furthermore was in a position to act on its contents. The obvious contact was the king's private secretary, Colonel

Clive Wigram. He was the only person concerned with the petition to raise the possibility of investigating its claims. When the War Office failed to respond to his suggestion, Wigram did not persist. In any case, it was a more of a comment than a suggestion.

Schwarz says he spent months working on his petition to the king, gathering facts and writing it. In a letter to the War Office of 8 August 1921 asking that it repatriate him, he reveals that in his preparation he was 'in communication with Australia collecting documents and verifying dates'. He does not disclose who his Australian contacts were or what documents he sought. Verified documents and dates would need to come from an official source. As we have seen, his 'dates' were not the highlight of his recollections. How he, still a registered deserter, could have gathered information from officials without revealing himself raises the possibility of collusion with well-placed sources in Australia.

In the early post-war years at Defence Department HQ in Melbourne, following the pardon, his AIF enlistment papers were taken out of the 'shame' file and worked over with handwritten notes and stamps to show transgressions had been either pardoned, they had not happened or if they had were to be forgiven. His AIF papers for 1915 originally showed he was struck off the strength of the 55th Battery Siege Brigade from Monday 25 October for being absent without leave (AWL). His British Army papers show he joined the Fusiliers on that day. A month later, an AIF board of inquiry had discharged him 'in consequence of desertion'. The Australian records were changed post-war to show he had been 'discharged in England and joined the Imperial Army both on 23 October', which was a Saturday.[11] Papers that would prove both official discharge and transfer do not exist in either country. They have never existed. Officials ruled through the line 'Struck off Strength having deserted'. They removed the details listing him as both AWL and an illegal absentee. A note was added beneath the deleted lines: 'All records of desertion to be expunged from this mans [sic] record. Granted Pardon. Vide Def. AB 452/3/699 6/10/21.'

'Cancelled' was stamped over the words 'Discharged in consequences of desertion, 1.4.20. To forfeit all rights of repatriation to Australia all service leave and monies'. A footnote read, 'Minister for Defence approves of the pardon for this soldier on the recommendation of the

War Office in view of his subsequent good service in the Imperial Army which he joined under the name MERRITT, two days after deserting the AIF.'[12] While another form (B.103) has mentions of desertion struck out to be replaced by 'Discharged in England. Joined Imperial Army 23.10.15 [*sic*]' (note, there is no date for his 'discharge' from the AIF).

A query from a public servant in his file (20 July 1921) asks, 'He gets no medals for AIF I take it?' The Defence Department advised the War Office that Schwarz did not qualify for Australian service medals, that the War Office must issue service medals it considered were due to him.[13] It did, awarding him the British War Medal and Victory Medal.[14] These documents emphasize the uniqueness of his story and the bizarre attempts to hide the truth. As for the original court martial that found Schwarz guilty of desertion, the Australian Archives was unable to produce a transcript or other details.

Other men of German origin did not encounter the discrimination Schwarz claimed he suffered. They found no reason to desert. They also performed heroic deeds: Lieutenant Edward Mattner MM, DCM, MC is a prime example.

The details in this chapter suggest collusion of persons with Schwarz's 'plans already made'. It is reinforced by the confidence on his part that he would succeed in achieving his goal. In the next chapter I offer a theory on who those helpers might have been and why they felt under an obligation that bound them and Schwarz to secrecy that has lasted to this day.

Postscript

Contrast the considered treatment that the British War Office gave Schwarz with that it gave to another original member of the 55th Siege Brigade's No. 2 Battery, Major William Tomkinson, of New South Wales, who asked in the early post-war years that he be considered for the award of the 1915-1916 Star, a service medal. Tomkinson began his career as a lieutenant with the battery. He had been handsomely decorated for his efforts, awarded the Distinguished Service Order (DSO) for bravery and the oak leaves that indicated a commander in the field had mentioned him in dispatches. He claimed the Star on the basis that in December 1915 he had been temporarily attached to a British artillery unit in France, the 27th Siege Battery. Officially he was the advance officer for the 55th, which was still at its base in England. In his application Tomkinson pointed out he had been taken on the strength of the 27th and shared the front-line risks with the other members of the battery. The War Office rejected the simple claim out of hand and in stark contrast to their dealing with Schwarz's far greater request.

The Defence Department took up Tomkinson's case. In a minute notice to the Military Board the department officer in charge of base records noted, 'We have Stars to burn … I am of the opinion Major Tomkinson has earned his ten times over … we have paid for the medals, so presumably, have some say in their disposal.' Apparently not. The matter reached the ears of Prime Minister William Hughes and a confidential cable was sent through his office to Australia House for passing on to the War Office. In it the Military Board asked that the War Office reconsider its decision, arguing that others who were not required to get near the front line, including members of the Red Cross and YMCA, were recipients of the Star. The War Office was not moved. It replied that 'temporary visits to a theatre of war do not qualify an individual for the award of the 1914/15 Star, and as this officer was sent to France on an instructional tour which was for temporary purposes only, he cannot be considered to be eligible for the aforementioned award.'

What it amounted to was a denial of a claim by a brave officer that he had been early in the front line. The War Office did not take up the suggestion of the Australians that it check the 27th's records to see whether Tomkinson's claims could be substantiated. There the matter has rested.[15]

Chapter 11

E Pluribus Unum
'I Would Like to Say a Lot, but Cannot'

The connection

In 1647, as England's Civil War drew to a close with the surrender of King Charles, his Controller of Ordnance, Elias Ashmole, moved from the Royalist capital, Oxford, to London. On the surface this was odd behaviour. Tension was still high between Royalist and Parliamentary forces. In any case, Royalist officers were banned from coming within 20 miles (32km) of the capital with the exception it appears of this member of the king's staff. 'Ashmole could not hope to go unrecognized,' Knight and Lomas write, 'so he must have had some guarantee of protection.'[1] He did. Ashmole settled in London, where he lived openly. Among his acquaintances were former enemies, including leading Parliamentarians. The authors surmise: 'There can be little doubt that this was due to the fact he was a Freemason … a fraternal structure in which Cavalier could meet Roundhead and Catholic could meet Puritan without fear and without malice.'[2]

In the following years Ashmole built an organization that became known as an 'invisible society'. It was to help make him 'one of the most important figures in the official history of Freemasonry'.[3] The society was a gathering of intelligent and influential men from both sides of the civil war topped up with like-minded individuals from other European centres. In 1662, with the restoration of the monarchy the organization came into the open as the Royal Society. Its patron and sponsor was, naturally enough, Charles II. Almost all its founding members were Freemasons.[4] Among the early Fellows of the Royal Society (FRS) were Sir Isaac Newton (1642-1727), the mathematician and scientist who defined the law of gravity, and the architect Sir Christopher Wren, who designed London's St Paul's Cathedral.

Ashmole's story has parallels and coincidences with Schwarz's. For example, both Ashmole and Schwarz felt secure in travelling to London when they were ostensibly men on the run from the prevailing law. Ashmole was supposedly at risk from the Roundhead army and civil authorities, Schwarz from the Army and civil authorities. Neither man behaved there as though they were fugitives. In fact, their actions were those of men confident they were under some form of protection. Schwarz says he spent the weekend he deserted in buying clothes. He had, as we have seen, registered at the Union Jack Club but most probably stayed openly at the address he gave to the Royal Fusiliers recruiters, 23 Warrender Road, Holborn. Both men went on to become lauded by the communities that once would have seen them punished. Both men were Freemasons.

When I first came to consider the possibility that Schwarz had helpers I assumed they had come from officers of both Australian and British armies who had sympathized with Schwarz's complaints of bias and his desire for front-line combat; they had quietly arranged his 'transfer' from the AIF to the Sportsman's Battalion. This assumption does not explain the story at the various levels in which it is played out. For example, the testimonies of Councillor Cairns and Headmaster Henderson; neither man was an army officer, nor was the occupant of number 23 Warrender Road, Islington, Charles Croucher. The statements of the first two in their references recommending him as a suitable candidate for officer training are, as we have seen, obviously false and were never queried. Officials do not appear to have bothered with Croucher or the residence in which he lived as the sole registered occupant.

When Schwarz's case reached higher levels – Buckingham Palace, Whitehall, the War Office and the Australian Government – his heroism on the face of it appears to have blinded all to the necessity of even a routine investigation into his claims, in particular the claim that reveals before deserting he had already made plans to do so. What were they and who was involved in his progress from vilified victim to deserter to hero to model citizen? We will never know for certain, although on the face of it more than a few sympathetic officers were involved.

I considered the possibility of a homosexual link. From his early teenage years, Schwarz, whose father died in his first year of life, spent much of his life among men. The cadet officers took a special interest in him, he says, because of his desire for a full-time military career. It was a time when ignorance of and hostility towards homosexuality meant that, much like Freemasonry, it operated under a cloak of secrecy; the scandal of revelation for a 'member' could mean prosecution, persecution, even death. I have been unable to find evidence that Schwarz or his helpers were homosexuals.

Another possibility, Schwarz's support group was based on his membership of the Church of England (Anglican). As we have seen, the church was promoting the Allied cause as a Holy War, a fight for freedom, honour and chivalry. The latter two attributes obviously appealed to a man who had taken as his middle name the legendary one of Lancelot. My speculation on the church and Schwarz led me inadvertently to another mystery in this story – the possible involvement of Littleton Groom, who was the Federal Attorney General at the time Schwarz returned to Australia. Groom was the member of the Australian Parliament for Schwarz's electorate, Darling Downs, a seat based on Schwarz's home town of Toowoomba, Queensland. Among Groom's other activities was his membership of the General Council of the Church of England Australian Synod. Had Schwarz's supporters in Britain been church members who wanted help from Australian authorities they had in Groom a powerful and influential figure to call on. The introduction of Groom into the story raised the possibility that while still using the alias Merritt, Schwarz may have appealed directly to the Attorney General, who was his local member. In his letter to the War Office of 8 August 1921, Schwarz reveals, that in preparing his petition to the king he was 'in communication with Australia collecting documents and verifying dates'. It is an extraordinary claim for a man on the run to make. He never disclosed, nor was he asked to disclose, who his contacts were or what documents he sought or was given. However, Groom firms as one possible source, the assumption being that Schwarz must have revealed his story to him before preparing his petition to the king. The two were born and raised in Toowoomba. Groom, born on 22 April 1867, was a short, dapper man, a familiar sight around his hometown. In 1901, Darling Downs voters had put his father into the first Commonwealth Parliament but he had died within the year. The father's backers turned to the son to fill the vacancy. Groom, a successful barrister, easily won the by-election to begin a parliamentary career that ended with his retirement in 1929. For his services he was knighted. Schwarz, in the post-war years, mentored a young man, Reginald Swarz, who was to win the Darling Downs seat in 1949 and hold it until 1972. His parliamentary career also earned him a knighthood. Schwarz's standing in the community at this stage of his life was such that, had he wished, he too could have had gone into politics. Instead he sought the quiet life ...

Groom had been in a position to acquire material Schwarz needed for his petition. He had been for some time during the war assistant Minister of Defence. Post-war as Attorney General he would have been able to smooth out legal matters that may have stood in the way of Schwarz's rehabilitation. The wartime Minister of Defence George Pearce had the responsibility of approving Schwarz's pardon. Obviously he worked closely with Groom in their various wartime roles and in post-war Cabinets. Quite possibly both men were among the high percentage of MPs who were Freemasons. This was an era when men did not openly reveal their membership of the society, except in secret handshakes as means of identifying, without asking, other members. Before agreeing to clemency, Pearce could have turned to Groom for details of his (Groom's) young constituent. They may have discussed Schwarz at some earlier time, mulling over why the enthusiastic young cadet corps officer who wanted a military career had disgraced himself by deserting.

A curious episode took place on the day Schwarz arrived back in Toowoomba to be greeted by a civic reception, at which Groom was an invited speaker. The two travelled up from Brisbane that morning on the same train. Yet Groom told the reception he had no idea Schwarz was on board. If true, Groom's electorate office had failed to keep him abreast of an important local matter. Most citizens knew of Schwarz's pending arrival and were out in the streets, at the station and outside the town hall to greet him. Groom, it appears, had made the long journey from Canberra for the occasion and most probably was on the same train as Schwarz for the overnight Sydney-Brisbane leg of the journey as well. Had they spent a night and half a day on trains, and not crossed paths? This leads to the assumption that Groom in his comment sought to distance himself from an association with Schwarz. Why? Any politician worth his salt seeks the reflected glory of a local hero. Are we to assume Groom was another of the young man's helpers who in doing so crossed legal barriers? Did he do it to help a constituent, a man of the same faith – or a brother Freemason? Groom is one of several possibilities as the man behind the 'Fair Play' letter published in the *Toowoomba Chronicle* after the war that revealed the story of Schwarz's wartime activities. The writer, who hides his identity behind the nom de plume, makes it clear he had known for years during the war that Schwarz was alive and fighting under an alias; that he was in touch with him and had offered help. Groom, as the current Attorney General, was in no position to come out publicly in favour of a law-breaker. However, given his influence in Toowoomba, he would have had no trouble in 'planting' the letter. That the writer was a mature person is suggested by use of the phrase 'young man', while a description of the petition as a 'deposition' suggests a legal mind.

While researching the subject of religion as an influence on Schwarz I was struck by problems regarding his professed denomination. As we have seen, he gave his religion in both the AIF and the Fusiliers attestation forms as Church of England (now Anglican). Yet the *Toowoomba Chronicle* report on his civic reception has a Congregational minister, the Reverend F.E. Adams, claiming Schwarz as a member of his flock. Adams had not met Schwarz before his return home. The minister had arrived in Toowoomba to take charge of the Congregational church in 1919. Ill health forced Adams to resign in 1924.[5] Schwarz may have copied the example set by another well-known Toowoomba resident of the time, George Washington Griffiths, owner of the town's foundry. Griffith gave up his Congregational membership and started attending Church of England services.[6] He was an active Freemason – membership of the Church of England and the brotherhood were mutually compatible at the time. Adams spoke publicly at the civic reception saying he was 'the minister of the church to which Lieutenant Schwarz belonged'.[7] Except for one detail Adams is another candidate as author of the anonymous Fair Play letter. The detail that casts doubts on this is that the letter calls his subject 'Leslie Walter Schwarz'. The transposition of given names suggests the minister was not close to the Schwarz family.

When Schwarz gave C of E as his religion on the AIF papers he signed to serve overseas, had he already made plans to desert? In other words, his change in denominations was a part of this plan. In any case, for the rest of his life Schwarz was a devout Anglican. He died on 9 January 1969 and was cremated 'according to Anglican rites', says a relative. A similar phrase appears in his official biography.[8] Possibly, the minister who conducted the funeral service was a forerunner of those clergy who today do not allow Freemasons to conduct funerals according to their rites in Anglican churches. Sections of the contemporary church oppose Freemasonry on the grounds that it does not comply with Christian doctrine.

Freemasonry is a fraternal structure in which, as noted earlier, 'Cavalier could meet Roundhead and Catholic could meet Puritan without fear and without malice.' During my research for Schwarz's story I received in the mail an envelope containing private papers of Schwarz's. They had not been sent to the Australian War Museum archives. Among them was a certificate of membership of the United Grand Lodge of Antient Free and Accepted Masons of Queensland. State lodges operated separately before the UGLAFAMQ was formed in 1921. Schwarz had signed the scroll as testimony that he was a brother. There are various dates on the scroll. Schwarz was still in England for all of 1921. Below Schwarz's signature the UGLAFAMQ Grand Master has signed that he affixed the seal on the scroll on 11 April 1924, in Brisbane. This scroll may have been issued as a replacement for one issued before the lodges united. The local lodge was the Southern Cross Lodge (Toowoomba) No. 18. Or did it replace one issued to Schwarz as Merritt? The Queensland scroll shows Schwarz had 'advanced to the second and third degrees'. A third degree lodge member is titled a Master Mason. We are able to assume that he started as a novice, an Entered Apprentice, the first degree. The next step was to become a Fellow Craft Mason, the second degree, followed by the third step, regarded as the pinnacle for most Masons.[9] Men of humble background such as Schwarz saw Freemasonry as a means of improving their status in life. Careers advanced at a much slower rate, if they advanced at all, for non-members. And Schwarz, as should be obvious by now, was ambitious.

Freemasonry capital

By 1915, Freemasonry was in its heyday in Britain. Swinging London had become the world's major centre of Freemasonry. There were an estimated 1,500 Masonic lodges in the empire's capital, more than in any other city in the world. As a fellow member of the ultimate secret society Schwarz would have been welcome in any of them. One writer depicts Masonry in Britain as a wide-ranging network of 600,000 contacts, a great many of whom are disposed to do favours for one another because that had been the main reason they had joined, to bring succour to a distressed Brother Mason.[10]

The ranks of the institutions of London were imbued with members of the brotherhood. They ruled its council (the Lord Mayor was a Mason, as were many aldermen and staff). Members were found in most fields of the city's activities. They were, and today in many cases still are, parliamentarians, civil servants, judges, lawyers, court officials, police officers, stockbrokers and insurance company executives. There were so many Freemasons in the financial heart of London, known as 'the City', that each bank in the 1-square mile area had its own lodge. Lloyd's Bank, for example, supported the Black Horse Lodge of Lombard Street, while the Bank of England's eponymous lodge dated back to 1788. Schwarz as Merritt at the recruiting station declaration gave his address as 23 Warrender Road, Holborn. This is in the Islington council area. A wartime lodge had been created a few streets away at the Great Southern Hotel, Islington, where the Sportsmen's survivors held a post-war reunion.

Freemasons were strong in the trades and crafts, the great produce markets – and the armed forces. All it would have taken from Schwarz to identify himself in much of London was the Masonic handshake …

Having claimed his age when enrolling with the Sportsman's was twenty-one he had overcome the need to have a parent or guardian's permission for his actions, including membership of the Freemasons. Most lodges would have accepted him despite his age had he claimed that his father, whom he had turned into a middle-class Englishman, had been a Mason. The question of age of admission has always been a variable. For example, the first president of the United States, George Washington, was initiated into the Fredericksburg Masonic Lodge five months before his twenty-first birthday on Friday, 4 November 1752.[11] Schwarz may have joined as an apprentice before the war in a civil or army lodge. The officers who helped him in his cadet years are more than likely to have been members of his local (Toowoomba) lodge. Their influence on him would, therefore, not have been solely with military matters.

An ancient Masonry rule law says: 'All Masons are as Brethren upon the same level …'[12] Accordingly, Schwarz could have expected to be treated as an equal by other members, including military officers. He was a Stranger Brother. Such men 'must be respected and if he is in want, [a member] must relieve him if you can or else direct him how he can be relieved; you must employ him, or else recommend him to be employed.'[13]

Traditionally the monarch is the titular head of Freemasonry in Britain. The current queen is its Grand Patroness. Although records do not show King George V, who ruled throughout the First World War, was a member of the brotherhood, his father, Edward, as Prince of Wales, continued the royal tradition by becoming the Grand Master of Freemasons. The Duke of Kent currently holds the title. We may assume George viewed the fraternity in a benevolent light and was subject to influence from his advisers, amongst whom were without a doubt practising Masons. Naturally, had Schwarz followed his father into a lodge he would have been subject to the ancient rules, including those cited here and taken from the rule book first published in 1723.

An argument can be made of help being extended to Schwarz from within the AIF through various levels of the British Army up to the War Council to the king's counselors, with further support from civil sources all in the name of brotherhood. This support continued into the post-war years. The Latin proverb quoted at the start of this chapter, *e pluribus unum* (out of many, one), signifies the status of brotherhood to the Masons.[14] Schwarz's membership may explain why the various officials he dealt with gave his background cursory, if any, checks: character was assumed of a brother. A further point, as we have seen, to enlist in the Sportsman's the applicant was required to personally attend its HQ based at the Hotel Cecil in the Strand for an initial examination and interview. Was it simple coincidence that the hotel was also the venue of a lodge? Did the two operate in ignorance of one another? We can almost certainly accept that lodge members took advantage of the proximity to approach the new battalion on behalf of a relative or friend, or themselves. Membership of the Sportsman's was keenly sought. With this acceptance we may have the answer to one of the major mysteries in Schwarz's story: why as a deserter did he enlist in the high profile Sportsman's over lesser known units in which, it would seem, his risk of discovery was not as likely? I argue he did so through his Masonic connection. It was part of his 'plans already made' before he deserted. While on the subject of mysteries, it is appropriate here to return to a mystery raised in chapter three: why the Battalion was given special dispensation to enlist men up to forty-five years of age, this in a battalion whose emphasis was on recruiting fit young men in the prime of life. This upper age limit was exclusive to the Sportsman's in the British Army. Given the above criteria it may be assumed that these mature recruits were considered to measure up to the younger men in physique and lifestyle. In other words, they were fit for active service and would do their bit when the time came. However, most of them were removed from service on the front line after a very short time, or 'left kicking their heels in England when the battalion moved overseas'.[15] It suggests some unknown but influential force was brought to bear on Mrs Cunliff-Owen and her fellow founders on behalf of a group of men who otherwise had little hope of donning the king's uniform.

As we have seen, Field Marshal Earl Kitchener, at that time Secretary of State for War, gave permission for the Sportsman's Battalion to be formed. The veteran soldier, statesman and diplomat was one of the military's notable Freemasons.

At a first reading of Schwarz's letter to the king, which accompanied his petition for a pardon, his offer to lose all his limbs in the king's service brings to mind the *Monty Python and the Holy Grail* knight who lost his limbs in a macabre act of bravado. However, as I worked on the Masonic material and its connection with Schwarz – and his adoption and stress of 'Lancelot', it struck me the hyperbole is more suggestive of a Freemason's oath. A member swears to accept as penalties for revealing the fraternity's secret ghoulish punishments, for example to have his tongue torn out, heart torn from his breast, bowels burned to ashes and the top of his skull sliced off for revealing secrets. Knight says, as the rituals themselves express it, the 'more effective penalty for doing anything displeasing to Masonry is to be shunned by the entire brotherhood, a penalty adequate to bring a man to ruin … in every profession and every branch of society.'[16] Hence silence.

I should mention here I put my theories to the United Grand Lodge of England (UGLE) and also wrote an article for the UGLE magazine outlining Schwarz's story and the facts that give it, by deduction, its Masonic connection. I finished by asking for comment or other information, opinion or suggestions from readers. This was some years ago. I do not know whether the article was used, but all I have had in return is silence. My theory, in summary, is that fellow Masons carried out their vows of obligation in relation to Schwarz by helping him move from the AIF to the Fusiliers, endorsing his candidacy for officer rank, pushing for his pardon and changing official documents to show he had not deserted the ranks of his country's army in wartime. This was a chain of related events that involved lowly ranked officers and officials, leading politicians and the king's advisers, if not the king himself. The silence of the brotherhood in this case has never been broken. Schwarz hinted at the vow behind this silence when he told his civic reception in Toowoomba, 'I would like to say a lot [about his experiences] but cannot.' He gave no reason. However, we may assume the initiates in the audience understood his silence. We may conclude that those who helped Schwarz felt their obligation as members of the world's oldest secret society was a higher duty than other obligations they had sworn to uphold.

Schwarz's idyll

A claim strongly argued in several books on secret societies asserts Freemasonry grew out of the Knights Templar. The knights divided themselves by rank and ritually kept secrets – not just from the public, but from each other.[17] The point to be made here is the connection between Freemasons and Schwarz embodied in his adoption of the name Lancelot, the legendary knight in the court of King Arthur. According to legend its members were under a vow to recover the Holy Grail lost by the Knights Templar

The fashionable Hotel Cecil in the Strand, where Schwarz, as Walter Lancelot Merritt (or sombody representing himself as Merritt on Schwarz's behalf), received his enlistment papers for the 1st Sportsman's Battalion. The hotel was also home to one of London's many Freemason lodges during the First World War. Did its presence have an influence on Schwarz's choice of battalion?

Was Schwarz, as Englishman Walter Lancelot Merritt, among this group outside this Sportsman's hut? He was, like other members of the elite unit, generally stronger, taller and fitter than the average Tommy.

Schwarz as a pre-war militia cadet officer with his mother, Augusta Wilhelmine (née Otto). (*Australian War Memorial*)

What is your Name? ... ... 1.

What is your full Address? 2. 23

Are you a British Subject? ...LONDON 3.

What is your Age? ... ...WHITEHALL 4. 21

What is your Trade or Calling? ... OCT. 1915 5.

Are you Married? ... ...10702 No

Have you ever served in any branch of His Majesty's Forces, naval or military, if so, state particulars? 7. No

7A. Have you truly stated the whole, if any, of your previous service? 7A.

Are you willing to be vaccinated or re-vaccinated? ... 8.

Are you willing to be enlisted for General Service? ... 9.

Did you receive a Notice, and do you understand its meaning, and who gave it to you? 10.

Are you willing to serve upon the following conditions provided His should so long require your services?

For the duration of the War, at the end of which

Two questions Schwarz answered untruthfully when he enlisted with the Sportsman's Battalion as Walter Lancelot Merritt. Months before he had sworn to 'truly serve our Sovereign Lord the King in the Australian Imperial Forces', the AIF then being a semi-autonomous branch of His Majesty's forces. (*Schwarz papers*)

"Daily Mail" WAR PICTURES   CROWN COPYRIGHT RESERVED.

WOUNDED "TOMMY" TO THE PHOTOGRAPHER: "I'M NOT A GERMAN!"

This wounded soldier, carried by other German prisoners, paradoxically utters the words that Schwarz in his guise as Walter Lancelot Merritt had to live by during his six long years as the son of an Englishman: 'I'm not a German.'

Details of Schwarz's award of the Military Cross, posted in *The London Gazette* supplement of 11 January 1919. (*Schwarz's papers*)

Certificate to note Lieutenant Merritt's Bar to his Military Cross, dated 13 November 1918. A month earlier he had carried for the second time a large flag in a brigade-strength advance on enemy lines to denote its centre. He and his party moved so far ahead of the main advance they captured twenty-eight Germans and held out under heavy trench mortar and machine-gun fire until the remainder of the brigade arrived. Schwarz was severely wounded. His citation notes: 'He behaved most gallantly and did fine work'. (*Schwarz's papers*)

Schwarz's mother wrote to the Australian External Affairs Department in January 1916 (she dates it 1915) asking for its help in tracing her son, saying she did not believe he would 'leave his ranks'. However, she must have been officially told by then that he had done so. The letter raises questions over what she, her family and friends did or did not know. (*Schwarz's papers*)

The tense and unsympathetic response from the Australian Department of Defence in January 1916 to the letter from Schwarz's mother in which she asked for help in tracing the whereabouts of her son. (*Schwarz's papers*)

The notation made by King George V on the document containing his petition to approve Schwarz's pardon for deserting His Majesty's Forces. It brought to an end his heroic career as Lieutenant Walter Lancelot Merritt MC and Bar. (*Schwarz's papers*)

An early photograph of the Cenotaph, London, shortly after King George V unveiled it on Armistice Day 1920. It was erected as a symbol to the 'Glorious Dead' of the British Empire who fell in the First World War. Relatives of loved ones are shown here laying wreaths and flowers at its base, a tradition that continues to this day. (*Photocrom Co. Ltd.*)

A page from Schwarz's Australian Army records showing the changes made following the King's pardon. Officials ruled through the line 'Struck off Strength having deserted'. They removed the details listing him as both AWL and an illegal absentee. A note was added beneath the deleted lines: 'All records of desertion to be expunged from this mans [*sic*] record'. Another form (B.103) has mentions of desertion struck out to be replaced by 'Discharged in England. Joined Imperial Army 23.10.15 [*sic*]'.

This lodge membership scroll signed by Walter Schwarz is evidence for the author's assertion that fellow Freemasons secretly helped and protected Schwarz in his guise as Walter Lancelot Merritt. (*Schwarz's papers*)

The Thiele brothers, left to right, Benjamin, aged twenty-two, Herbert, twenty-four, and Ewald (pronounced Evald), twenty. As members of 43rd Battalion Australian Imperial Force. When it came to fighting they were loyal to king and country and relatives said that, unlike Schwarz, they experienced no discrimination because of their heritage. Herbert and Ben were both seriously wounded and Ewald was killed in action. Herbert lost both legs. Despite this handicap in the post-war years he was so energetic and mobile that people were often surprised to find he was a double amputee.

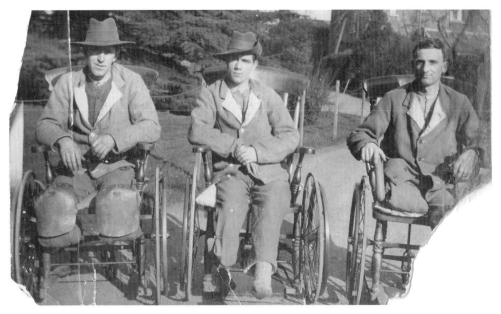

Herb Thiele (right) with two other amputees recovers in an unnamed English hospital.

This unsourced photograph was published in volume five of *The History of the Great European War its causes and effects* under the following caption: *GERMAN PRISONERS ENTERING THE CAGES. A careful study of many of these German soldiers will show that they present aspects of unmistakable 'degenerate' type; they contrast badly with the clean, alert British soldier. All bear their misfortune with a certain air of enjoyment and no doubt relief.* The ten-volume set was part-published during the war. The caption serves as stark evidence of the pressure Schwarz, in his pose as an Englishman, was under should he have been exposed as one of those 'degenerates'. It also helps us understand the frustration, anger and humiliation Maximilian Mügge expresses in his *The War Diary of a Square Peg* at the treatment meted out to him and other men of German heritage no matter how distant or whether they had fought for Britain against their 'cousins'.

On 4 February 1938 Schwarz and Charlotte (Lottie) Maud Hart (both pictured) at St Thomas's Anglican Church in the Brisbane suburb of Toowong. Picture shows Schwarz negotiating the church steps with his prosthetic right leg. (*Schwarz's papers*)

The Australian War Memorial, Canberra, Australian Capital Territory, depository of individual and official war records. Schwarz had instructed on his death that his medals, including the official Military Cross and Bar, not be sent here but to the Royal Fusiliers HQ at the Tower of London. Here they were 'very grateful indeed to receive them'. (*en.wikipedia.org, reproduced under GNU Free Documentation License*)

Schwarz could not have chosen a more appropriate knight to emulate; Sir Lancelot was the noblest and most virtuous of them all, prepared to lay down his life for his king and, for that matter, Queen Guinevere. Sir Thomas Malory in his *Le Morte d'Arthur* (1485) writes tournaments, battles, and adventures were Lancelot's priorities, necessitating he remain single lest marriage thwart the pursuit of an adventurous knighthood.

Lancelot chose to perform deeds of gallantry and chivalry in disguise, making sure the king eventually found out so that he would forgive Lancelot his deception, which had been, after all, for the greater good.

Lancelot was admitted to Arthur's court at the age of eighteen – the same age as Schwarz was when he too took up arms in the service of his liege, King George V. The myth tells us in:

> all tournaments and jousts and deeds of arms, both for life and death, Lancelot passed all other knights, and was never overcome … and he increased marvellously in worship, wherefore Queen Guinevere had him in great favour, above all other knights. And for certain he loved the queen again above all other ladies; and for her did many deeds of arms and saved her from peril through his noble chivalry.[18]

It may be interpreted from the myths the love between queen and knight was unrequited, a further sign of Lancelot's chivalry. As Lancelot worshipped his queen, Schwarz may have come to idolize Queen Mary as a fair lady whose life he would slay all manner of men and face all perils to protect.

Schwarz's worship of Queen Mary may have been revealed in the story he told his family of a private meeting at which Mary had given him a personally embroidered supper cloth, telling him to take it home for his mother. Schwarz said the meeting took place at Buckingham Palace on the day the king personally decorated him. In the Crimea and Boer wars, Queen Victoria knitted and crocheted scarves, mittens and undercoats for soldiers. If Queen Mary had decided to carry on the tradition with her own handiwork it came as a surprise to one First World War expert when I mentioned it. He knew of no records to show the queen gave personal gifts to those attending the palace for investiture ceremonies – or at any other time. When the king pinned the medal on his chest Schwarz was still Lieutenant Merritt, as such the queen would have not had a particular reason for picking him out among the award recipients for a private meeting. But as Schwarz, a man pardoned by the king, the queen's interest is much more likely to have been piqued by a desire to personally hear at first hand his incredible story. The gift, therefore, became her personal recognition of his gallantry and an expression of understanding and sympathy for his long-suffering mother whose Germanic roots the women shared.

Schwarz may have woven the meaning of the meeting into his Arthurian fantasy: the supper cloth is much like a scarf in shape. In his mind it became Mary's personal tribute to a brave knight – as was Guinevere's gift of her scarf to the original Lancelot, the man who had fought all manner of enemies to uphold her honour.

The fate of the supper cloth/scarf is not known.

Chapter 12

'A True Australian, not a German'

On 7 September 1915, seven weeks before Walter Schwarz deserted, another young man with a German name volunteered for service with the Australian Army. It was a week before his twenty-second birthday. At the recruiting office in Adelaide, the capital city of South Australia, he filled out an attestation form under his own name, Edward Mattner. He had been eligible to enlist without his parents' consent from the age of twenty-one. Unlike Schwarz, Mattner did not see his future in the Army. Yet he was to become one of the most decorated Australian soldiers in the First World War. On the Western Front he won, in order, the Military Medal (as a corporal), the Distinguished Conduct Medal (as a sergeant) and the Military Cross (as a lieutenant), all for personal bravery in the field. He was wounded in action but remained on duty. In later years he served as a long-term member of Federal Parliament.

By the latter part of 1915, community feelings against local Germans had become intense, a major reason being the arrival of the first long list of casualties from Gallipoli, where the Anzacs had been pinned down for six months. Contrarily the same list made it obvious to the Army's top brass they could no longer continue to copy the British Army's practice of rejecting out of hand men whose names suggested German or Austrian origin.[1] Despite the official ban, recruiting officers in Australia early in the war had passed as eligible young men of non-British origin who had fought and died on Gallipoli. Others with German bloodlines had enlisted by avoiding the race bar in various ways – they had anglicized their names: Johann became John, Wilhelm, William, Friedrich, Frederick or Fred, Carl, Charles, Heinrich, Henry, while Schmidt had become Smith, Schwarz, Black (although not in all cases) and so on. Sons of German-Australian mothers who had married into British families bore the paternal and anglicized first names. Some surnames were at best ambiguous – Edward Mattner's, for example. Men changed their names in the wartime rush to naturalization; others did so on enlisting, including Hugo Ludolff, who enlisted as Albert Neil.

The only hint that there were doubts in Mattner's mind that the ban still existed is shown by the fact that he cited his mother, Mrs Emily Louisa Mattner (née Hocking), South Australian-born daughter of English migrants, as his next-of-kin, that is, the person to be notified should he be killed or wounded. Like Schwarz in this matter he had lied on his attestation paper. Under army regulations a single male was required to identify his father as next of kin should the father be living, and Mattner's father was. Although known as William Charles, his father had been christened Wilhelm Carl. A study of the records of other men of German background shows that this practice of naming the mother as next of kin was not uncommon, particularly if the mother had a British or British-sounding name.[2]

Mattner was an Adelaide University graduate, the first member of his family to have had a tertiary education. Unlike Schwarz's, his qualifications were genuine. He was due to set out on a career as a schoolteacher. The South Australian Education Department had appointed him to the staff of Port Pirie High School. He could have moved north to the rural school and seen out the war. A refusal to serve would not have made him an exception. Official figures show enlistments in the First AIF for eligible men between eighteen and forty-four averaged less than 40 per cent.

Setting aside what he had worked and studied to achieve to risk life and limb on the other side of the world and against men who shared his ancestral heritage appears, on the face of it, illogical, if not foolish. Family members claim his reasons were anything but facile. They point out his father as a young man had refused to speak German for the rest of his life because he considered himself a 'true Australian, not a German'. This same consideration, together with a sense of duty, was, they say, the reason the son enlisted.[3] In the Second World War it led him to again take up arms and, post-war, to accept a senate seat.

Mattner played top-grade cricket for the Adelaide University and Australian Rules football with the South Australian National Football League team, Unley. His army medical records show he was a strapping specimen, just short of 6 feet in height (2.28m) and weighing 159 pounds (72 kg). He was, in brief, a prize catch. Having been found fit for active service he swore, as Schwarz had done, under his own name to 'well and truly serve Our Sovereign Lord the King and resist His Majesty's enemies and cause His Majesty's peace to be kept and maintained, so help me God'.

Mattner's grandfather, Carl Wilhelm, was a comparatively late arrival among the German settlers to South Australia. As we have seen, they had been coming from shortly after white settlement in 1837. Carl, the first-born child of Johann Friedrich Mattner, was twenty when he landed in 1857. He was born at Lagow, in Brandenburg, Prussia, and had learned from a man named Schultz to be a wheelwright. He practised this trade in the township of Lobethal, in the Adelaide Hills, a popular district for Germans and their descendants. On 4 September 1862, he married Pauline Emilie Marks, the second child of Carl Christian Marks and Caroline Wilhelmine, née Rohrlach. She had been born in Germany and arrived in South Australia with her parents. She grew up in the Adelaide Hills village of Hahndorf (whose name was forcibly changed to Ambleside in the First World War) and went to its Lutheran school. Wilhelm Carl, Edward's father, was born in 1865 in the Hills town of Harrogate (formerly Harrowgate). He married 'outside', to a woman of Anglo-Australian parents: Emily Hocking, the daughter of Edward James Hocking and Mary Anna Tonkin, née Stephens. The couple had four children: Ruby, Maud, Edward and Leo, in that order. Edward was born on 16 September 1893. The couple lived initially at Harrogate, where Wilhelm (William) worked as a carrier. He later bought a property at Oakbank, in the Hills district, where he ran a mixed farm. He set an example of public service that son Edward was to follow. He represented the Oakbank Ward of the District Council of Onkaparinga from 1921 to 1929, when he died. He was council chairman in the last two years of his life.[4] Edward received a conventional state school education at Oakbank Primary and Adelaide High School before attending the University of Adelaide.

As a raw recruit Mattner was sent to the base infantry depot, Glen Osmond, an Adelaide suburb. After basic training he joined the 18th Field Artillery Battalion, the first South Australian field battery to go on active service in the war. Along with the 16th, 17th and 106th from other states they comprised the 6th Artillery Brigade, which was part of the AIF 2nd Division. Each battery was made up of three or four 18-pounders. Like Schwarz, Mattner left Australia with the lowly rank of gunner, the brigade embarking from Melbourne on 22 November 1915, arriving a month later at Suez. In early January 1916, Mattner was appointed acting bombardier and two months later was on his way to France with the rank of bombardier. In the next two years he was to fight through the Somme, Pozieres, Bullecourt, Messines, Ypres, Menin Road and Passchendaele battles, more promotions quickly following.

Mattner was decorated twice in the fighting at Ypres. The deeds that brought him his first decoration, the Military Medal, give us an initial impression of a character whose calmness and courage under fire was to last until the guns fell silent on Armistice Day, 11 November 1918. The citation:

At Ploegsteert on the 1st June 1917, these NCOs and men [Corporal E.W. Mattner, Bombardier W.C. Chambers, Gunner W.J. F. Sage, Gunner R. Hindes, Bombardier C. Fulgrave] under the orders of Major E.T. Dean, while the 18th Battery was being heavily shelled, displayed the greatest bravery and devotion to duty in extinguishing on three separate occasions fires which had broken out from the hostile shelling in three gun pits of the battery and in several ammunition dumps. While the gun pits were on fire, and the ammunition in them and several dumps surrounding the battery were exploding, they brought buckets of water to the battery commander, who was standing on top of the pit being dealt with and worked in the pits with him putting out the fire. They consequently put out the burning dumps. On more than one occasion boxes exploded while they were handling the dump. On the pits again catching fire under the heavy shelling they returned in the face of it and successfully renewed their efforts. Their disregard for personal safety, fine devotion and determination undoubtedly saved the guns and a large quantity of ammunition, 1,000 rounds only being destroyed out of some 5,000 stored at the pits.[5]

Major Dean, in a letter to supporters of the battery at home, commended the men who supported him: 'Never once when I asked them to go with me did they hesitate and they have been given truly their just reward.' He goes on to say that a few nights later he was sitting in an old building listening to an artillery barrage. As it moved closer he left the building – it was about 1.30 am and pitch dark – with the intention of moving his men to a safer position. The moment he stepped clear:

> a big shell went in and blew the chair I had been sitting on to bits and buried ... two boys. Fulgrave and Mattner went back with me and we got the boys out, but the building was blown down on top of us and several times we ourselves were nearly buried. We got them [the wounded two] away ... after this I collapsed and Fulgrave took me to the brigade headquarters. Unfortunately I've been unable to go back since. I asked the colonel to recommend both Fulgrave and Mattner again for their devotion and bravery this night, but I have heard of no result yet but I am proud of them and their conduct.[6]

Shortly after this, Mattner was promoted to temporary sergeant.

A South Australian newspaper, *The Register*, published the following details on 22 September 1917:

> Mr and Mrs W.C. Mattner of Oakbank have received information that their son, Sergeant E.W. Mattner, of the 18th Battery Australia Field Artillery, was awarded the Military Medal on June 7 [*sic*]. He was one of five volunteers who extinguished fires in their battery position and saved three guns and 15,000 rounds of ammunition [*sic*] thus preventing many casualties.

His second award came in September, the Distinguished Conduct Medal for conspicuous gallantry and devotion to duty. The DCM was first awarded in the British Army in 1854 and until the Military Medal was introduced in the First World War was the only award for bravery for men below officer rank. The citation in this case reads:

Awarded Sergeant Edward William Mattner, 8th Army (Brigade), Aust F.A. (Division), 1st Anzac Corps. On the morning of the 16th September 1917 at Hooge, when the battery was engaged in firing a barrage over our troops it came under heavy fire. The battery commander was wounded and a gun and detachment knocked out, the men all being killed and wounded, and another gun was set on fire. Sgt Mattner, pending the arrival of another officer at the control station took charge, got the wounded away and kept the battery in action, showing the greatest determination, force of character and ability. He exposed himself fearlessly to the hostile fire and lifted the battery out of its difficulty at a critical moment. He was awarded the Military Medal on 30th June 1917.

It is signed by Brigadier General William Napier, 1st Anzacs.[7]

On 12 October 1917, Mattner was promoted in the field to second lieutenant. A fortnight later came his third decoration, the Military Cross. The citation reads:

On 27th Octr, 1917, near Zonnebeke a party of infantry came under very heavy fire near his battery position. One man was killed and seven were wounded. The shelling continued incessantly for half an hour, but he at once collected a party of four men and went out to rescue them. With the assistance of these men he dressed all the wounded and removed them to a place of safety. It took them fifteen minutes to do this and during the whole of the time they were under heavy shellfire. He was slightly wounded but remained at duty.[8]

Promoted to first lieutenant in January 1918, he subsequently became adjutant of the 6th Brigade.

In March that year he preceded Schwarz by two years in attending Buckingham Palace, where the king pinned the MC on his chest. Mattner did not mention any of his awards in his letters home, except for the personal presentation of his MC. He is understood to be one of only five Australian soldiers personally decorated by His Majesty, not, of course, counting Schwarz.

Two more stories on Mattner appeared in *The Register*. Both mention, without citing a source, that he had received a Bar to his MC. On 3 December 1917, it noted:

Second lieutenant E.W. Mattner, son of Mr and Mrs C. Mattner of Rockdale, Oakbank, has been awarded the Military Cross. He left Australia as a gunner more than two years ago, attached to the 18th Battery Field Artillery. During the last six months he has won the MM and a Bar [*sic*], the DCM and his commission, and the Military Cross. Advice received from the military authorities on 14 November stated that Lieutenant E.W. Mattner was wounded slightly and remaining at duty.

The third report appeared on 7 February 1918, under the heading 'A Fine Achievement':

One of the proudest of the many fine batteries on the Western Front in France is a battery of the Australian Field Artillery which left Australia in charge of an officer who has been mentioned in dispatches five times, wounded once and gassed twice. To the end of October last the battery had gained forty-one decorations and thirteen commissions had been secured by non-commissioned officers and men. The officer alluded to who is at present commanding an artillery brigade in France is delighted with the achievements of the battery and of its individual members, particularly Second Lieutenant E.W. Mattner ... whose mother is Mrs E.L. Mattner of Oakbank. As corporal, this young officer won the Military Medal and Bar [see below] as sergeant the Distinguished Conduct Medal and as second-lieutenant the Military Cross. He left Australia as a gunner and in due course, on the field was successively promoted to bombardier, corporal, sergeant and second lieutenant. In twenty-seven months of active service he has not missed a day on duty, notwithstanding that he was wounded in October ... every act for which he was decorated was for personal bravery under very heavy shellfire. The OC considers that this splendid record is unequalled in the Australian Artillery and probably the British Army.

Reports of his receiving a bar to the MM have persisted over the years. Family members say neither Mattner's parents nor other relatives were its source. However, it may have arisen from Major Dean's letter to the 18th Battery Club in Adelaide of 1 July 1917, written, as we have seen, weeks after Mattner had been awarded the MM. A club member may have passed on Dean's second recommendation to a reporter and in the process 'recommendation' became fact. Years later, the then Senator Mattner asked the Department of Defence records office for a copy of his MM citation, pointing out copies of his 'other two citations' had been sent to his mother during the war. She had since died and he now held those copies.[9] The records office replied in a letter addressed to him at his Commonwealth Parliament offices in Adelaide, 'It is regretted a copy of the Citation covering the action that earned you the Military Medal is not available.'[10] The point of this exchange is twofold: 1. Mattner states he won the MM, MC and DCM. He does not claim to have been awarded a Bar to the MM or, indeed, to the other medals; 2. this important military document did eventually turn up and is today in his service record papers.

Throughout the war, no matter how fraught the circumstances, Mattner wrote home constantly. He posted more than eighty letters to family members starting with a description of the voyage to Egypt in 1915 and continuing until the end of the war.

His daughter, Mrs Margaret Crisp, told the author: 'We found Dad's letters after his death – we wish we'd been able to talk to him about them. They are family letters of reassurance, never details of the fighting, just occasionally, "we have been very busy", though after the Armistice he describes the Hindenburg Line assault.'

In 1916, showing his farming background, he mentioned in one letter, 'Strawberries ripening in a lovely countryside', and in another his pleasure in hearing his sister had named her new baby Edward William. In 1917 he asked his mother, 'Please deduct £1 4s 6d out of my allotment toward Leo's education at Roseworthy Agricultural College. He must have his chance at education as I had. He needn't know about it.' Leo, his younger brother, was born in 1902.

A letter in 1918 described the hardships of the French villagers and also this insightful comment on a man whose ancestry was, like his, Prussian, the commander of the Australian forces:

Sir John Monash is a grand fellow. He is not a professional soldier. He is a shrewd keen engineer who realizes how men should be treated. So if we are out for winter resting, his idea is not to drill, drill, drill us – no, he says give men an education, give them fresh outlooks and they will be keener soldiers.[11]

Mattner did not return to Australia until 1919, when he was honourably discharged in October that year. In addition to his bravery awards he had earned the 1914-1915 Star, the British War Medal and the Victory Medal.

In 1920 he bought a farm at Balhannah, in the Adelaide Hills. At first glance Balhannah may have sounded suspiciously foreign to those who had been intent on wiping out Germanic place names. But the name is unique, made up by early settler James Thomson, Hannah being the name of both his mother and sister and 'Bal' the Gaelic word for town, although another source says it was a corruption of 'Belle', for beautiful.[12] Crisp said the family was never aware of anti-German feelings in their district, except for that reflected by the name changes of towns and railway stations. She did recall, however, how her grandmother, Emily, Edward's mother, had run into bias when she attended a polling booth to vote in the 1917 conscription referendum. 'She was told to put her vote in a separate box because of her German surname – presumably they were to be discarded,' said Crisp. 'She refused, pointing out that she was born in South Australia of English parents and more particularly as her son was away in France fighting for Australia.' Emily died in 1920. As with his letters, Crisp said, 'Dad didn't talk about his wartime experiences to us children – just a few tales of funny happenings.' One example she recalled: 'It was learned that there was a General Mattner in the opposing German Army and Dad's mates in his 18th Battery joked, "Hey, Ted, tell your cousin to stop sending over those bloody shells."'

In the post-war years Mattner became an early pioneer of summer potato cropping. He also ran a dairy herd, raised fat lambs and grew subterranean clover. In 1923 he married Lorna Prince of Peterborough, South Australia. They had six children: Margaret, Barbara, Phillip, Richard, William and Charles. Mattner took a keen interest in civic affairs and served as an office bearer in a number of community organizations. He was president of the Onkaparinga branch of the Agricultural Bureau, secretary and president of the Balhannah and Oakbank area school committees, secretary of the Onkaparinga district committee of the Liberal and Country League political party and president of the Onkaparinga Returned Soldiers' and Sailors' Imperial League of Australia. He was made a life member of the South Australian Agricultural Bureau. He attended the local Methodist church.[13]

In 1940, aged forty-seven, the Army called him back to service as area officer in Balhannah with his wartime rank of lieutenant. He was soon promoted to captain, then major. July 1941 found him on board the passenger liner *Queen Mary*. It had been refitted as a troopship. On it he sailed, as he had done in the First World War, for Egypt, this time taking reinforcements to the 2/43rd and 2/48th battalions. He discovered there were insufficient lifeboats for the numbers on board, so set the men to build rafts and a ramp from the lower decks at the ship's stern to give them more chance to abandon ship if torpedoed. Water was also in short supply for shaving and baths, so he organized the troops in lines at one end of the swimming pool, had them jump in and gave them three minutes to make their way to the other end before the next line of men went in.[14] He was back in Australia before the end of the year and attached as second-in-command to the 13th Field Regiment, which was posted to New Guinea. Crisp recalled, 'He told our mother that it broke his heart to take such young boys, not fully trained or equipped, into those terrible conditions.' Within months he had become a casualty himself. Invalided home and admitted to hospital, his records show a diagnosis of fibrositis, a painful condition that causes difficulty in movement. With the illness lingering, he was found to be permanently unfit for further service and placed on the Army retired list on 25 June 1942.

A few years later his life took another unexpected turn. He agreed to warm a seat in Federal Parliament for the Liberal Party when a senator resigned unexpectedly. But first he had to be formally selected by a joint sitting of the two South Australian Parliament houses. Being foisted on the voters without going to a poll is not considered the best way to start a political career and it appeared Mattner proved the point when he lost in the 1946 general elections. However, his war experiences obviously inspired him to rally and rejoin the fray. Standing as a candidate in 1949 he regained the seat and went on to a distinguished parliamentary career. In 1951 he was elected President of the Senate, a position he held until 1953. He retired on 30 June 1968.[15]

Away from Parliament his interest in racing led him to breed successful racehorses at the farm, including Resting, Sebago and Wyclass. A committee member of the Onkaparinga Racing Club, he had the pleasure of seeing Sebago win a Great Eastern Steeplechase at Oakbank. After the death of his wife in December 1970, he went to live in Woodside, yet another Adelaide Hills town, next door to his youngest son, Dr Charles Mattner. The wartime hero and senate president died in December 1977. He and his wife are buried at Bonney's Flat Cemetery, Balhannah.[16]

The extensive history book of the Mattner family in South Australia, published in 1980, mentions only briefly Edward's parliamentary career and ignores altogether his outstanding military career. In fact, military deeds in general seem to have been avoided in the histories of the family's various branches, although there were many volunteers among them. When I mentioned this to his great-granddaughter Katherine Daniell, she responded: 'In the past, I believe he wanted to forget about the war. He very rarely talked about it. He never made any attempt to have his war efforts written about.' The family does have his documented records and family history. 'Members of the family are now interested in learning about him,' Daniell explained. Charles Mattner adds: 'At first he did not tell family members about his experiences in the war, but he later relented a little to give a few details of the horrors and carnage in France.'

Daniell, a brilliant young student, won the 2004 Sir John Monash engineering scholarship. At the presentation ceremony, the words her great-grandfather had penned so long ago and so perspicaciously in one of his letters home were read out: 'Sir John Monash is a grand fellow. He is not a professional soldier; he is a shrewd keen engineer who realizes how men should be treated ...'

Annual Anzac Days – in which the wartime service of Australian and New Zealand forces are commemorated – and the 18th Battery picnic reunions were special to him and his family. The picnics were held each year on 22 November, the date on which the battery sailed from Melbourne in 1915. Big reunions of Edward and Lorna's extended family were held in 1994 and again at Christmas 2004. Their six children attended both events. Members of the younger generation were able to read Mattner's First World War letters.

Mattner himself may have approved of the fact that his deeds have not been glorified outside the family. He was not a man to dwell on the past. He lived a full and worthwhile life, a man who served the community in war and peace. His story brings a dose of reality to the Anglo-centric view of the Anzac legend.

'You forget he had no legs'

I cannot end this section on 'good' German Anzacs without mention of the three Thiele brothers: Herbert, aged twenty-four, Benjamin, twenty-two, and Ewald (pronounced Evald]), twenty in 1915. Together they add a further dose of stark reality to the German Anzac legend. Their parents were both German-born. They raised the three boys and two daughters, Olivia and Marta, on their farm on South Australia's lower Yorke Peninsula. Their mother spoke little English and the family conversed with her in German. The state government had granted land to the boys with the proviso they clear it for agricultural use. They had only partly completed the task when the Army took them. According to Herbert's daughter-in-law, Mary Thiele, throughout the war government notices were posted to them warning they would lose the land unless they completed clearing it for agricultural use. The fact that they were otherwise engaged was not considered an acceptable excuse and they lost the allotment.

In the Armentières sector Herbert and Ben were among the first 43rd Battalion troops to see action. They were both seriously wounded, Ben on 1 March 1917. Ten days later he had reached the Wandsworth General Hospital, London, where he received further treatment for the gunshot wounds he had sustained to the lumbar regions, the lower left leg and thigh. Ben had been ill in hospital when the 43rd entered the line late in December 1916 and rejoined it in January. Herbert was wounded in April on the outskirts of Ploegsteert Woods, Belgium. According to one account, his legs were 'blown off, one below the knee and the other above, while almost all his body was peppered with fragments of a shell which burst near him.'[17] Family legend has it that British corpsmen took a look at his injuries and left him for dead. French first aid men found him and carried him to a casualty clearing station. Herbert was later to recall the station as a place where his limbs were dropped into one of the baskets filled with amputated legs and arms – including both arms and legs of a fellow soldier. Herbert was evacuated to Whitstable Hospital, England. Repatriated to Australia he was given a medical discharge in September 1918. Ewald was one of the battalion's thirty-six Other Ranks killed in action on 4 October 1917. He is buried at Zonnebeke.[18]

The family had grown up as Lutherans. But that changed when their pastor who brought the news of Herbert's injuries to the family concluded by saying, 'Perhaps it's just as well because Herb would not have given up dancing.' Herbert had been a keen dancer, a pastime forbidden by the strict Lutheran churchman. As a result of the insensitive comment his sisters became Methodists for the rest of their lives.

After the war, Herbert, not happy with the prosthetic legs with which he had been fitted, made himself a peg leg, which he said gave him greater stability. This leg had a flap enabling him to fold it when he sat in a church, theatre or grandstand. For the rest of his life he used a walking stick, but few realized the energetic sportsman had good reason for doing so. Despite the handicap, Herbert led an active life in the post-war years. As the eldest of the two surviving brothers Herb inherited the small family farm on Yorke Peninsula – and expanded it by 300 acres (121ha). An accomplished horseman before the war he became a well-known figure in the South Australian horse-trotting world. For three consecutive years he was the state's leading owner-trainer. It began when he swapped a farm horse for a third-rate pacer. He won minor country events and bought more pacers at bargain prices. Practically all turned out trumps. His best buy was a gelding, Black Hope, in 1937. He paid fifty guineas (AUD $105) and won £2,000 (AUD $4,000) in stake money.[19] His daughter-in-law, Mrs Mary Thiele, recalls Herb as an energetic man: 'You forgot he had no legs, he did everything a normal person would do.' She remembers him climbing a ladder onto to the sloping roof of her home to attach a hood he had made for the chimney.

Herbert lived to the age of seventy-nine. His brother Ben, who had also been seriously wounded, settled in Yorketown, on the Peninsula, and worked as a mechanic. Ben was a gifted musician and made his own violin. He and his sons, also musically talented, played at local dances and concerts.

One cannot help feel that George Angas, the chairman of the South Australia Company, was prescient when he campaigned in the nineteenth century to bring God-fearing Germans to Australia. He gave them the taste for freedom and prosperity, virtues later generations defended with their lives in two world wars.

Chapter 13

'The Queerest Battalion in the British Army'

The British War Office subjected male residents of German origin to harsh and discriminatory treatment throughout the First World War. It is a shameful and all but forgotten chapter in the history of war. My original reason for exploring this line of research was to find comparisons between the British and the Australian treatment of those men who served – or wanted to serve – in their forces who had German bloodlines. A further reason for my interest was to imagine a scenario in which Schwarz would have been treated had he, as his falsified records show, resigned from the AIF and legitimately enlisted in the British Fusiliers – under his German name.

A search in the usual places – libraries, Internet, war archives – proved all but fruitless until I came across a brief reference in *Dismembering, the Male Men's Bodies and the Great War,* published in 1996. It gave me the lead into the elusive subject. Its author, British academic Joanna Bourke, mentions in passing that First World War British soldiers with German bloodlines were removed from the front line and placed in the 33rd Battalion Midshire Regiment (also known as the Kaiser's Own).[1] However, fellow academic Hew Strachan, the Chicele Professor of the History of War at Oxford, in a criticism of what he described as Bourke's 'somewhat inchoate book', wrote that her comment was an example of her failure to distinguish fact from fiction. He went on, 'She does not always realize when she is having her leg pulled. She seems to think … that the 33rd Battalion Midshire Regiment (Kaiser's Own) really existed.'[2] Strachan, a distinguished Oxford historian, was mocking my rare lead. Bourke, a lecturer in economics and social history at Birkbeck College, University of London, cites as her source the book by linguist and man of letters at the time Maximilian Mügge, *The War Diary of a Square Peg*. Published by G. Routledge & Sons in 1920, it is a little-known work long out of publication. I wrote to Bourke asking whether she was in a position to enlarge on her comment regarding the existence of such a regiment. She did not reply. In the meantime I had acquired a copy of *Square Peg*. The detail in Mügge's book led me to the conclusion that the War Office did create a non-combatant regiment of German-origin men, most of them British citizens, either naturalized or by birth. It is best to make clear at this stage that despite Mügge's often whimsical use of names, the labour battalion in which he and others served was part of the Middlesex Regiment, dubbed by him the Midshire Regiment. Among those forced into its ranks were decorated heroes, long-service soldiers of the Regular British Army and men who had been wounded in action. I wrote to Strachan pointing out that Mügge had accurately quoted a report in *The Times* that confirmed the existence of such a body and that the book had been seriously reviewed on publication without doubt being cast on its authenticity. Strachan had, I should emphasize, made his comments about Bourke's work en passant. He was good enough to reply, initially admitting he had not read *Square Peg*. Nevertheless he felt 'the whole thing is a spoof, albeit one that is pretty sophisticated.' He went on to say that although he did not personally 'know of the existence of a labour battalion made up of men of German origin in the First World War … that seems to be an entirely logical explanation of the evidence which you have unearthed.' He added, 'My only reservation is a concern why more attention has not been drawn to such a labour battalion before this. The Chinese labour battalions that worked for the British Army in 1917-18 are reasonably well-known. Why no consideration of a labour battalion made of German origin?' Indeed.

The irony behind the ill-treatment of these men of German origin is twofold. Firstly, like Schwarz, many of them wanted to fight for Britain and the empire. Had they done so they would almost certainly have proved loyal and competent soldiers. In fact, some of them had been withdrawn from the battlefield because of their antecedents and placed in the battalion. Secondly, British society was replete with men of similar ancestry, from the king down, through the aristocracy, Parliament, the law, medicine, finance, arts and so on. As we have seen, neither the king nor his cousin, the First Sea Lord, was immune from anti-alien hysteria.

Mügge, like Schwarz, experienced at first hand the lot of a man willing to serve his country to the best of his considerable abilities but was prevented from doing so because, although he was born and bred in England, he was of Hanoverian ancestry. The War Office could have utilized his talents in a number of ways: he was a linguist, so his services would have been valuable as an interpreter, censor or interrogator. His general knowledge of Europe, and of Germany in particular, would have made him an asset to army intelligence. Instead, as a member of the 'aliens' regiment, he was put to work as a labourer, sweeper, scullion, toilet cleaner, policeman, target setter, trench digger, clerk … anything that would ensure his assets were not utilized for the war effort.

It soon becomes obvious from his writings that the ban on 'aliens' serving in the British forces was imposed with far more vigour than was the case for Australia. While it was of an unofficial nature within the Australian Army, a special provision in the British Manual of Military Law stated that an alien may be enlisted only if 'His Majesty think fit to signify his consent, through a Secretary of State [government minister].' It goes on to say that an alien 'shall not be capable of holding any higher rank than that of warrant officer or non-commissioned officer.' It was another law broken by Schwarz under his alias.

Square Peg in relation to Schwarz shows what would have been his fate had his real name been at any stage revealed. His decorations for bravery would have counted for nothing. He would have ended up with Mügge, an enforced non-combatant, doing menial tasks for the duration. And what could be more menial for a fighting man than assignment as mess orderly, a task Schwarz writes he was given after being removed from his gun crew for no apparent reason other than his name.

Mügge's account is by no means a detailed history of the battalion. It appears one does not exist in official records. We do learn that members of the battalion gave themselves the nickname Bing Boys.[3] It came from a West End company that staged popular revues starting with *The Bing Boys Are Here* in 1916, followed by *The Bing Boys Are There* the next year and *The Bing Boys On Broadway* in 1918. In the 1916 revue the enduring song *If You Were the Only Girl in the World* was given its first airing.

Mügge's 'record' comprises in the main diary entries. From them emerge the thoughts of a man trying to make sense of his and the world's predicament. The jottings on matters that take his interest amount to a mixture of personal opinions, experiences and observations, extracts from newspaper articles, documents and legal opinions relating to naturalization. He slips effortlessly into French (never German) uses Greek and Latin phrases and cites Greek and Roman history, myths and legends, a natural affectation for a man of his scholarship. Mügge has a whimsical attitude towards names, mixing the factual with the fictitious. For example, the town of Reading becomes Albrickham, the latter a name coined by Thomas Hardy for the town in *Life's Little Ironies*. (In *his Jude the Obscure*, Reading (Albrickham) appeared again.) The Bing Boys' camp, Mügge dubs 'Camp Barmy' (the original Barmy Army?). He records a Bing Boy who leaves camp every evening in a taxi for the George Hotel, Reptum (*sic*). At 9.15 pm sharp every morning, his taxi comes to the hotel to fetch him back to camp. On the other hand, he talks of the anguish of men withdrawn from the front line and posted to the battalion, 'boys who had volunteered to fight for England, the land of their birth ... their mental sufferings were dreadful. There are no words adequate to ... express one's opinion ...'[4] Overall his writing is a mixture of humour, tolerance and the occasional caustic remark as his frustration boils over at the injustice of it all.

His diary begins with the outbreak of war in August 1914 with the words:

> The fools! The unutterable fools ... It is inconceivable. These two great nations [Britain and Germany] whose alliances would have guaranteed the peace of Europe if not the world.

Mügge appears not to have made an effort to enlist within the first year of the war. He was thirty-six and had a bad heart. He would not have been classified as A1 (fit). He confined himself to his writings and comments on the treatment of those with German roots in civilian life. A friend of his was dismissed from his position as senior classical master at a grammar school where he had taught for seven years. 'Like myself, my friend is a British subject of Hanoverian origin,' he writes. 'Ancestors of his had settled in this country hundreds of years ago.' His fellow teachers had shown 'a stony indifference'.[5] In September 1915 he offered to join a Voluntary Aid Detachment (VAD) unit. Its members carried out first aid and nursing duties. He was turned down. 'As usual, the name did it,' he writes. 'And it is quite useless apparently to refer to one's citizenship.'[6]

The following month, after a London recruiting station rejected him for enlistment into the Army, he wrote to the man in charge of recruiting, Lord Derby, at the War Office (between 1916–1918 Derby was Undersecretary, then Secretary for War.):

> I am perfectly willing and most desirous to do all I can for the safety of our country fighting for its existence ... I should deem it a duty and an honour to be permitted to do something that contributes directly and immediately to the needs of the country. [He would be] very grateful indeed if he [Derby] would give me an opportunity of repaying the great debt I feel I owe to England, the home of civic liberty.

Lord Derby did not respond, prompting Mügge to write in his diary:

> A naturalized British subject who does not happen to be a Privy Councillor or related to royalty becomes a person *capite minutus* the moment the country of his birth goes to war with the country of his adoption.[7]

In February 1916 the War Office did ask him to come in. Its staff orally tested his fluency in several modern languages, all of which he passed.

> A club friend who knows one or two of the Whitehall deities, however, tells me not to be disappointed if I hear no more ... He says that the gutter-press would howl itself into hysterics if I were given a job in the Intelligence Department or even only the Interpreters' Corps. My friend knows that only a few years ago Whitehall referred to me as a 'scholar of eminence'...

He did hear from the WO. A letter informed him he would be allowed to join the Army but only as a private and he would have no chance of a commission.

By late March 1916, Private Mügge was in basic training camp, rising with younger and healthier volunteers at 5.00 am each day, cleaning out their hut, touching up their uniforms and assembling for a forty-five minute parade before breakfast followed by the first of several route marches. 'We are dead-tired at the end of the day,' he wrote on 7 April 1916. 'My heart gives me a lot of trouble but the war-machine is ruthless. And I am sure my troubles are nothing compared with the boys' terrible ordeal in the trenches.'

On 18 April 1916 he wrote again to the War Office asking for a transfer, reporting that his heart was worse. In response he was posted to No. 8 Company, Home Service Only, a labour unit whose motto was 'how to dodge work and be happy'. Among his duties were looking after the toilets and scrubbing floors for the 3rd Royal Southshires Camp.

By May, apparently with the help of some officers with whom he was friends, he was transferred to a non-combatants' corps he identifies as the 16th Royal Musketeers, 'a kind of dumping ground for conscientious objectors and ... naturalized Englishmen.' He was its only non-conscripted member. He was advised not to tell the others his name was German. Of the COs, he says, 'I cannot help admiring these pioneers of a far distant future, when the principles of humanitarianism will no longer be contrary to the natural disposition of man.'

It was in August 1916 that he was posted to what he called the 33rd Battalion Midshire Regiment, officially an infantry works (IW) battalion. Mügge understood it had been formed the previous month 'at Balmy Camp, Sussex'. It comprised men of German origin. As well as its self-imposed nickname – Bing Boys – it also acquired the further unofficial title the Kaiser's Own. Realizing the significance of the battalion, he notes:

When I had recovered from the first shock and regained my breath I turned to the paleface clerks in the orderly room tent and said, 'I take it this is not a regiment at all! This is a political concentration camp.'

'Hush, hush you mustn't say such a thing,' exclaimed a horrified staff sergeant. One of my tent mates who had arrived from a fighting unit a few hours before me was crying bitterly half the night. He was English bred and born, spoke no other tongue but that of Shakespeare, had volunteered in

1914, and been wounded in the Mons retreat and here he was, as he cried, 'Treated like a b... Hun!' It was heart-rending to listen to that boy's agony, his sighs and curses and groans ... All the men of German descent were recalled, except those who had fallen in the field of battle.[8] Regimental Sergeant Major Barker was the only non-commissioned officer in the regiment who can boast of pure British blood unpolluted by any Hunnish strain.[9]

In my research I confirmed James Macpherson, then Parliamentary Secretary to the Undersecretary for War, inadvertently or otherwise revealed the existence of the Germans-only battalion on 22 March 1917 when he told the House of Commons, 'Men of German origin and association were formed into a labour battalion the previous June.' Macpherson, who became Undersecretary of State for War (1918-1919) and was raised to the peerage as Baron Strathcarron of Banchor, went on to say it was incorrect to describe the members of the battalion as volunteers; they were conscripts in the ordinary sense of the term. The two companies of the battalion that had been sent to France had not been and would not be placed in the firing line; but it was too much to ask that those men who were able bodied and capable of strenuous work should not be used as a labour battalion apart from the firing line. He could not promise that other companies of the battalion would not be sent abroad to be employed in work behind the lines.[10]

Mügge writes that Macpherson's comments had angered himself and fellow members of the battalion. There were, in fact, a goodly number of volunteers in the battalion. He was one of them. 'What the boys who have actually been in the trenches say just now about Macpherson defies my unblushing pen,' he writes. As for the men all being fit for hard work, there were a considerable number of low category men (less than able-bodied) in the battalion. He concludes, 'I may add ... we have men who hold the DCM [Distinguished Conduct Medal], awarded for bravery in battle.'[11]

The day Macpherson made his contentious claims, in the House of Lords Lord Galway asked what the approximate number of women of enemy nationality now in England was, and whether the government would consider the desirability of deporting them with a view to reserving the food supplies of the country for British use. Viscount Sandhurst in reply estimated the number was between 22,000 and 23,000. Of these, some 12,000 were British-born. (Therefore, one would have thought, this qualified them as being of British nationality by birthright.) Sandhurst also said a large number of the remaining 10,000 or so had been resident in Britain for thirty, forty and even fifty years. Sandhurst indicated that the latter group had chosen to remain in Britain and, he went on, 'Many of them had sons fighting in the British Army.' His statement is at odds with that made by Macpherson on that day and with Mügge's account of the treatment of men of German origin. His statement would suggest several possibilities. Firstly, if accurate, not all able bodied men of German origin had been withdrawn from the firing line by 1917, nine months after the German labour battalion had been formed. Secondly, the reason these women chose to stay is obvious; they regarded Britain as their home, whether born there or having lived there for much of their lives. Thirdly, Sandhurst was not about to reveal that the sons of these women were not being allowed to defend their home. On the latter point, Sandhurst may not have been unaware until that day of the existence of the Bing Boys' battalion and the discriminatory policy behind its formation that Macpherson had revealed in the other chamber. He would not have been alone. Sandhurst concluded his reply by saying in so many words that the enemy women did not eat enough to be deported. Besides, the ships that would be needed to deport them were otherwise engaged.[12]

Earlier, London's *Evening Standard*, under the headline 'Queerest Battalion in the British Army', commented:

The problem of what to do with the enemy alien Britons seemed beyond the powers of the Army … Quite a number tried to attest but were met by refusal from recruiting sergeants who told them that they were not eligible for the British Army … With the coming into force of conscription the position of the enemy-born had to be considered by the War Office. It might easily be very dangerous to have them in the fighting line: dangerous possibly to Britain if the men attempted any 'comic business' when at the front, and dangerous also to the men who, if they were captured by the Germans, would assuredly be shot as traitors to the Fatherland. On the other hand, to allow them to remain free to enjoy war wages when pure Britons had to sacrifice their homes would have been grossly unfair to the latter. The War Office solution to the problem was to issue a general order that recruits of enemy descent were to be posted to the Midshire Regiment, and thence sent to a labour battalion of that regiment. And a strange battalion it is. There are men of every variation of accent, their proximity to the true British standard being more of less judged by the facility with which they manage the letters 'R' and 'W'. The man who can manage 'Around the rugged rocks the ragged rascals ran' three times without sounding like fizzy water is entitled to sergeant's stripes. The men are stated to be quite loyal – at least as far as can be outwardly judged – and contrary to common rumour, they do not talk German among themselves.

Mügge is light on statistics and his use of the terms 'battalion', 'regiment', 'company' and 'unit'. This presents a difficulty in estimating the strength of the German-origin battalion and, along with other relevant records, the information seems to have gone missing. One of the few indications of its size comes in his mention that 500 of its members were sent to work as labourers in France in March 1917. In the First World War British Army a battalion comprised 800 to 1,000 men, comprising four companies of up to 250 men. In battle, regiments did not serve together as a single unit. Rather, battalions of several regiments were assembled into a brigade comprising four battalions.[13]

Mügge found one note of pleasure: the cooking was excellent, far better than he had eaten in his previous postings. The reason, the German-origin cook was a chef from a leading London hotel. However, in the same note he goes on:

There is in my tent a poor creature, can't walk at all; rheumatic gout; had to be carted here. Born in England. Appeal Board chairman on being pointed out utter inability of man, alleged to have said, 'Oh they will find some work for him and he will be amongst his brother Huns.' Another man with two gold stripes [a gold stripe was awarded to a soldier each time he was wounded in action. They were worn laterally on the lower left-hand sleeve of his tunic] arrived today. Another b––– Hun who fought for England and was wounded for the cause of liberty.[14]

Mügge divides the Bing Boys into three categories:

(a) British born. Parents either naturalized British subjects of German descent, or actually Germans resident in Great Britain. Usually only father 'tainted'. These boys almost without exception pure English types; in speech character and appearance. Facial contours interesting proof of maternal preponderance (Vast majority of English mothers)

(b) Naturalized British subjects

1. Perfectly acclimatized specimens; appearance often, language almost pure English. Absolutely loyal.

2. Imperfectly acclimatized specimens. Speech usually more or less tainted or even broken. Sympathies now often wavering; result of persecution.

He writes: 'I presume the action of the Government in forming this "regiment" was partly due to the existence of a few doubtful individuals ... but I am convinced that the number of such doubtful individuals has been at least quadrupled by the stupid policy of isolation.'[15]

His entry of 27 August 1916 quotes an un–named but 'well-known journalist's article' on Germans who, like Schwarz, had chosen an anglicized alias:

The fact that they are lurking under British names does not makes them Britons ... Every German, no matter how respectable and successful and plausible he may be, stands convicted of one unpardonable crime: the crime of being a German. It is no excuse to say that a German cannot help being born a German; the same defence might be used for a viper or a rat!

Mügge comments, 'Well done, Sir! Excellent, I like that viper and rat touch.'[16]

Mügge writes that the Bing Boys included men of wealth, such as the man cited earlier who commutes to and from a hotel to the camp by taxi each day. 'Another fellow, Lockman, arrived in camp with several boxes, two kit bags, air pillows a gold-handled stick and an umbrella. Looked exactly as though going on a holiday.' A hairdresser inmate is granted regular weekend leave to do the hair of the Queen of Portugal. A Joseph Surface:

> rides about in two cars, a Rolls-Royce and a runabout, and lived in rooms that, though he was a private, would have ruined a lieutenant ... a most charming man, an MA of Oxford he has the ingratiating mellifluous accents of a fashionable club secretary and can talk about everything under the sun from Lloyds – where he makes some more money – to Lourdes. The son of a b— Hun 'naturalized or otherwise' as the papers elegantly phrase it, is nevertheless very patriotic ... [he has] made numerous friends among the officers through dining and driving them out [in] the Rolls-Royce.[17]

Despite their varied backgrounds, most Bing Boys were willing workers.

> Political outcasts they work nevertheless, so well, their output excelling that of any other unit by 100 per cent, that the authorities of the Ordnance Depot are clamouring for more and more of these efficient and persevering workers ... Day after day they load and unload, stack and unstack mountains of boxes and bags with a thousand and one things; liqueur glasses for officers' messes, gigantic limber carriages and forests of tent poles. They have nothing but their dry rations, two slices of bread with a slab of leathery meat and their flask of tea. Yet they work with a will ... despite the long hours, they are subject to endless parades in the evening and often it is late as 9.00 pm before they are allowed to rest.[18]

Mügge reports that a Bing Boy, sent as advance agent to arrange quarters for a move to Albrickham camp, was arrested as a German spy masquerading in a British uniform. 'It took quite an hour's hard work to set the poor thing free.'[19] On a less flippant note he records the London-born chief draughtsman of the Inland Revenue Department was at first exempted from conscription when the department claimed he was absolutely indispensable. However, when this view was attacked in the press, he was forcibly enlisted. 'He assists me occasionally in picking up matches (sweeping and draining the garden) while his former colleagues hold commissions and continue to draw part of their salaries.[20]

One of the most pleasing personal and public achievements of the Bing Boys was the formation of a concert party, which gave performances for charity and in hospitals to cheer the wounded. The *Albrickham Observer* noted after a performance at the Palace Theatre, it had assisted in raising money for several good causes. 'Its "really good orchestra" is under the direction of Lance Corporal Kuhr (late bandmaster of the West Yorks Regiment).' Mügge notes that despite the fact the public knew the performers were 'b--- Huns', its reception was excellent.[21]

In July 1917 Mügge was given the task of setting up a regimental institute, basically a recreational club. He went about the job with enthusiasm and enterprise. He writes:

Rich men in the regiment donated funds liberally to set up the finest equipped [club] in the whole of England. Walls were hung with excellent pictures, comfortable armchairs, free notepaper, newspapers, games, including cards and two billiard tables. Great pianists among them Hulf, Schumm [and] Lowry lived at the club to take advantage of the magnificent instruments provided. Whist drives, lectures, concerts were regular events.[22]

His entry for 9 July 1917 mentioned that the *Daily Chronicle* reports:

Disgraceful scenes took place in Highgate Hill on Saturday night when a mob of boys and women attacked the shop of Mr S. Kurz, which stands at the corner of Brunswick Road and Highgate Hill. All the windows were broken and the fixtures in the shop smashed up.

The business of a baker has been carried on here for many years by Mr Kurz who, although born in Germany, came to England 40 years ago, and has been naturalized for 21 years. Mr Kurz is highly respected, has two sons in the British Army, and his third son has been exempted on medical grounds.

A crowd of women began to gather outside the shop about half-past eight and began to shout and groan. They were soon joined by boys and young men, who threw stones, empty bottles and iron bolts at the windows.[23]

Commenting on the fact that a company from the regiment is to be sent to France as a working party Mügge writes: 'The French, I heard, objected to any Huns – not related to the Royal House [*sic*] or belonging to the ranks of knights or international financiers.'[24]

On 14 March 1917, Mügge came across a communication addressed 'Officer Commanding 33rd (Aliens) Midshire Regt.'. He described it as authentic proof of the status of the battalion 'with its Contemptibles, Mons men and long-service soldiers. [This is a reference to men of the pre-war Regular Army who fought in the first major battle of the war at Mons in August 1914.] English bred and born they offered their services in the beginning of the war and were considered good enough to form the first bulwark of defence. How many Bing Boys died in France; they were good enough for that?'

Examples of other entries:

4 October 1917: Repeating his claim that the Bing Boys were not a regiment but inmates in a political concentration camp, he shows a hint of bias himself. 'The other day, a German, fifty years of age, was given the alternative – internment, or the 33rd Midshires. His choice was the latter. I have nothing against the man. But we who volunteered to fight or work for England, we who are English citizens …!'

13 December 1917: 'There are three Contemptibles in our detachment. All Mons men and professional soldiers. Gerber (eight years' service), Noroock (eight years), Sax (twelve years). It is only right to state the authorities stripped a lance corporal in Dawnhill camp for sneering at these boys as "b-- Huns"!'

15 January 1918: '[Gerber] went out to France in August 1914, was wounded twice and fought like a British "lion cub" does – recklessly. Then the armchair soldiers discovered – after he had been out twenty-nine months – that the wicked Gerber was of "hostile origin" though born in England and he was hurried out of France and bunged into the 33rd Midshire.'

9 July 1918: 'They are still unearthing boys of German descent in France. We have quite a number of men here now with three and four chevrons.' (Mügge is obviously referring to service chevrons rather

than those worn by NCOs. One chevron was awarded for each year of
service – red for 1914 service. The stripes were worn on the lower right
sleeve of the tunic as an inverted V.)

21 August 1918: He notes: '*The Daily Telegraph* reports:

> Organized by the National Party, a demonstration to be followed by the
> presentation of a petition to the prime minister will take place in London
> on Saturday for the purpose of urging the internment of all enemy aliens,
> naturalized or un-naturalized. The demonstration will assemble inside
> the Marble Arch entrance to Hyde Park at 2.30 pm and speeches will be
> delivered by Brigadier General Page Croft, MP, Captain Tupper, Mr Leo
> Maxse, Mrs Dacre Fox, who was a parliamentary candidate for the seat of
> Richmond, Mr J. G. Jenkins and others. A resolution is to be submitted
> calling for the internment of all aliens of enemy blood.

'It has been sent all over the country in petition form and more than
1,000,000 signatures have been obtained ...'

In the same entry he writes of a 'delightful walk' with colleagues
Sommer and Merule to Punchball, 'a gigantic basin-like dale of
amphitheatrical shape ... which would seat comfortably 20,000 if
arranged for a National Opera Open Air Theatre ...' His companions
'collected a few pounds of raspberries and strawberries in the woods.'

30 Nov 1918: 'A man with four gold-stripes and the Mons ribbon,
Furtwängler was born in Scotland, recalled from France and stigmatized
by being put into this unit. When he begins to burr about the damned
politician who put him into this mob after all his noble service in France,
it is just as well that Whitehall is far and cannot hear. I do not think
Furtwängler will go out again if he can help it.'

11 Dec 1918: 'The boys of the regiment who served throughout the 1914
and 1915 campaigns, some of whom were wounded themselves, who
saw Bing Boy comrades die ... were very angry when they read what
Mrs Dacre Fox [see 21 August, 1918 entry] told the *Weekly Dispatch*
[8 December 1918]. We had great difficulty in preventing half a dozen

boys with gold [wounded in action] stripes from going to London and talk to the lady.

'Fox said: "We must clean our public life of German influence absolutely. By eradicating German influence. I mean getting rid of German blood. As a nation we are quite efficient enough to manage our own affairs without the aid of any enemy alien ..."

'On the subject of clearing every Boche out of this country the women are very earnest – much more it seems to me than some of the men.

'When they say every Hun they mean every single one of them. Not alone the military prisoners and the civilian prisoners interned in this country, but the naturalized Hun who has been buying British War Loans and subscribing with great ostentation to our charities. We don't want them or their gold.

'I do not accept either those Huns whose sons' names have appeared in our casualty lists. For one thing, they never ought to have been allowed to join our army.'

A month after the war had ended Mügge writes that from its inception in 1916 the colonel (of the aliens battalion) stood by:

> whilst the boys grew sulky under the insults of political ruffians and military bullies. He took no effective action when they suffered through vile innuendoes of a perfectly unscrupulous press, the most abominable dictatorship a country ever had. The result was inevitable ... Colonel Byle [*sic*] was disliked and many boys hated him ... Yet the record created by these Bing Boys, these political outcasts, was extraordinarily good. You could not withdraw the slightest detachment of them anywhere without the local military authority kicking up an awful shindy. After the withdrawal of the BB, double the number of men would be needed and then the work was done indifferently. These are facts for which I can vouch. And I have heard in France the BB, once away from the disgraceful stigma of the 33rd Midshires label, have been doing most excellent work.[25]

15 Dec 1918: 'Cohen showed me a communication marked secret. Urgent telegram to all OCs [officers commanding] to note that:

(a) alien enemy subjects
(b) British-born subjects of enemy origin
(c) naturalized British subjects of enemy origin
(d) coloured subjects

are not to be admitted for re-enlistment in the New Army.

'Am wondering what Consax, Furtwängler, Dieland senior and others of our crowd who were regulars before the war will think about it? The three men I mention all come under (b) and Furtwängler has been wounded four times …'

With the rush to demobilization, the Bing Boys came to the bitter conclusion that they had been forgotten as a force. They were not among the thousands of war-weary men and women being discharged into civilian life, and they had not been given an indication as to when this might start to happen. In January 1919 they held a meeting that resulted in their delivering a letter to the camp commandant. Mügge was one of the three men who composed the letter. It complained that the failure to release the men back into civilian life was a further case of bias. The letter goes on:

> Should the policy of differentiation be due to the composition of the personnel of this unit, we respectfully beg to point out that this unit comprises:
>
> (a) Regular and Territorial soldiers of pre-war days
> (b) Voluntary enlisted men prior to conscription [introduced in 1916]
> (c) Men under forty-nine who, owing to the incident of foreign parentage, were when called to the colours, denied the privilege of choosing their own units.
>
> any of the men in classes (a) and (b) have seen active service and have been awarded military decorations, and some have been wounded. They have subsequently been transferred compulsorily to this battalion under War Office instructions.
>
> The NCOs and men of this unit … are entitled to the same opportunities for release as other units of the British Army.[26]

When this failed to move the powers, the Bing Boys accepted Mügge's advice to appeal to the king's uncle, the Duke of Connaught, 'whose father was a German by birth ... is theoretically in exactly the same position as [us].' (Connaught was the third son of Queen Victoria and the German-born Prince Albert. An Army veteran, he had reached the rank of field marshal in 1902. Between 1911 and 1916 he was Governor General of Canada.)

In part the formal appeal reads:

The undersigned whose legal position owing to the incident of German parentage resembles that of Your Royal Highness, beg most respectfully to approach Your Royal Highness with the humble request most kindly to intervene on their behalf, since they have failed to obtain redress through the usual channels open to them.

Born in England, the petitioners were loyal British citizens throughout their lives, and on the outbreak of war volunteered for the Army. They, and many others of a similar status, served abroad with distinction and a number of those who joined were killed in the field.

Contrary to the spirit of British fairness they were, however, penalized and taken from their original units, compulsorily and against their will transferred to this battalion, where they were and are being treated like 'aliens'. While the war was in progress their loyalty to king and country constrained them to submit to the indignity of being labelled 'aliens'.

Now that hostilities have come to an end and since there is no longer any danger of assisting the enemy through a censure of the British Government, the petitioners consider it their duty to expose the small clique in the War Office responsible for the outrageous policy pursued. Your Royal Highness will, no doubt, remember the word of Cicero on the occasion of the impeachment of Verres:

In this single fact of their citizenship they feel they shall be safe ... take away this confidence, destroy this safeguard, you are shutting up against us all the world!

Being British citizens the petitioners claim to be on the same footing as the men of any other unit and are convinced that Your Royal Highness will most graciously take the necessary steps to stop the unconstitutional practice at the War Office. This practice of treating us as 'aliens' and deliberately delaying our demobilization is calculated to prejudice England's proud position in the League of Nations ...[27]

Within a week the duke had acted. As a result, Mügge writes, the 'ban was lifted at once and to the great joy of all concerned, the demobilization of this unit is now in full swing. Treated like any other unit of the British Army ... all the 1914 and 1915 men and those above thirty-seven years are going.'

Mügge, who qualified under the latter category, returned to London on 25 February 1919, where he 'shed the khaki uniform for good. I am a civilian again and feel as bewildered as a moth fluttering round the flame. My hair is getting grey.'

In the early post-war period a fellow BB member, the distinguished economist Henry Meulen, who had managed to write and have published his treatise 'Industrial Justice through Banking Reform' during the war, wrote a despairing letter to Mügge. Meulen was publisher of *The Individualist* (a periodical published by the Personal Rights Association) and a prominent member of the British free banking school, whose members argued unsuccessfully for the abolition of the privileges of the Bank of England and the extension of the Scottish 'free banking' system to the rest of the United Kingdom. In his letter to Mügge he expresses his disillusion with the way he has been treated by his fellow Britons:

I find myself singularly disinclined for reformish things these days. The fact is I don't like my fellow man as much as I did. His combination of vicious spite and stupidity has got on my nerves. I am more than ever determined to get out of the Government service ... and make money in some form of commerce. It seems to me more important to protect myself from my fellow man than to seek to help him in these days ...[28]

The New Age edition of 27 January 1921 carried a review of *Square Peg*. The un-named reviewer took the opportunity to attack the 'virulent anti-alien campaign within the Army and the community generally', describing it as a chapter in English history that no one can afford to forget or to remember with anything but humiliation. The un-named reviewer says Mügge's plight 'illuminates in a flash the idiocy of the whole anti-alien' campaign. Mügge, he insists, had good ground for railing, but he chose instead to interest himself in the work he had to do and the men he had to mix with. As a result he 'retains the dignity of a man of letters amid circumstances that he would have been justified in regarding as a deliberate insult.'

The reviewer further uses the column to attack press baron Lord Northcliffe (1865-1922), publisher of the UK *Daily Mail* and *Evening News*, as being primarily responsible 'for the fomenting and focusing of the instinctive English hatred of "foreigners"'. Northcliffe not only drove the country mad against 'aliens' but effectually deprived the poorer ones of their legal rights. He was the man who condoned the criminal excesses of the mob in the name of 'patriotism' and who popularized the phrase 'Once a German always a German'. The column went on:

> he not only made fools of us but of himself. His idea of a strong nation has always been that of a frenzied mob ... When we look back and remember the looting of the property of anyone who bore an unusual name, when we remember that the protection of English law was denied to English subjects, when, what was worst of all, the abilities of the English subjects were refused employment at the behest of [Northcliffe] the only possible prescription for us is sackcloth and ashes.

It is the nature of mass hysteria that it dissipates once its cause is removed, leaving wiser counsel to both reflect and prevail. Schwarz's fellow citizens in Toowoomba were a prime example of this changing mindset. The same spirit of reconciliation emerged surprisingly quickly in most communities whose members had in wartime persecuted neighbours in whose systems ran 'alien' blood. There came a combined hope that persecutions would be forgotten or forgiven. The issue that emerged from this anti-alien hysteria was the nature of citizenship itself, whether under certain circumstances it can be revoked at the whim of politicians or the clamour of native-born citizens of the predominant group, whether it guarantees the same rights for the sons and daughters of the persons granted it or who inherited it as their birthright.

The issue had earlier been canvassed in a post-war article in *Nation* in an editorial whose views are as relevant for countries such as Britain and Australia today. Extracts:

> Many emigrants [who] left the Fatherland to escape the Prussian system found in Great Britain freedom and opportunities denied to them at home. They liked our life and ways, settled here, became naturalized British subjects. They never formed a group apart. They merged themselves completely in their new environment. Not a few of them rose to high positions in diplomacy, commerce the public service and Parliament. When war broke out between the land of their birth and the land of their adoption, they sided overwhelmingly with the country where all their personal interests and associations lay, where they had made their home, where their children had been born.
>
> Throughout the war the naturalized British subjects of German birth have been absolutely loyal to Great Britain and the Allied cause, the exceptions to the contrary being so few as to be wholly negligible. Their sons ... have fought and died as volunteers in the British Army.
>
> It cannot be said that as a nation we have done much to smooth the difficult path of our fellow subjects of enemy birth. They have been made to feel themselves objects of suspicion and distrust. We have not availed ourselves of even a tenth of the services they stood ready to render. The popular attitude towards them has been too much governed by newspaper sensationalism. No British statesman has known how to address them ... There has been a campaign of innuendo and proscription against them ... Is it really the sober judgment of the country that the covenant of naturalization should be treated as a scrap of paper, to be altered or torn up as the Home Secretary of the day may think best? If so we are nearing a turning point in British history. No European nation has owed so much in the past as we have to a succession of alien immigrations. The day on which we in Great Britain narrow our vision of such problems to the standpoint of a niggardly nationalism will mark for posterity the beginning of our decline.[29]

Square Peg appears to have been Maximilian Mügge's last publication. His first, *Heinrich von Treitschke* (the German historian, 1834–1896, with strong nationalistic views), was published in 1896. In 1914, its publishers, Messrs T.C. & E.C. Jack, commissioned him to write a short monograph of Treitschke. Suspecting the reason for the request, Mügge comments, 'There must be whipping boys.' His second book, *Friedrich Nietzsche*, was first published in 1900, with several subsequent editions, the last in 1912. Published in 1916 were his books on Serbian folk songs, fairy tales and proverbs (the Serbs were on the Allies' side in the First World War).

In the introduction to *Square Peg* Mügge gives his address as 'The Royal Sussex Regiment, Fort Hill Camp, Newhaven'. He adds the date, April 1916, although the book did not appear until 1920. As if to emphasize his British roots he mentions notable ancestors Galfridus Mügge, Member of Parliament for Guildford in 1414, and Daniel Mügge, the King's Commissioner in 1538, and ironically quotes Theodor Mügge, an early nineteenth-century author, who wrote: 'Nowhere else on this earth is the Individual legally so well protected against all violence as he is in Great Britain.'[30] One source, the online Open Library, gives Maximilian's birth date as 1878. It does not show a date of death and I have not found a biography of the man in several reliable references.

Postscript

Further proof for the authenticity of *The War Diary of a Square Peg* came with a search of the individual war records of some of those Labour Corps members Mügge mentions. For example, the Scottish-born Edmond Furtwängler had enlisted with the 2nd Argyle & Sutherland Highlanders, moved to the King's Own Scottish Borders, then the Royal Hussars before being recalled from France, where he had served with distinction since November 1914, and then posted to the Middlesex Regiment's labour battalion in June 1915. As we have seen, Mügge comments, 'I do not think Furtwängler will go out again if he can help it.'

Mügge mentions briefly a Lowry. A search of the name reveals one of the most blatant cases of the War Office boffins sending men arbitrarily to the Labour Corps. They include the following Lowrys who had served in France before being withdrawn and posted (the regiment from which they were removed at the time is in brackets): Francis (Royal Field Artillery); George (service corps); James (Royal Irish Rifles); John (Royal Dublin Fusiliers); Joseph (Border Regiment); Maurice (Lancashire Corps); Stewart (Inniskilling Fusiliers); Thomas (Royal Irish Rifles); and William (Veterinary Corps). Other Lowrys were posted to the Labour Corps from their original regiments before they had a chance to join the fighting. Another, William, was posted to the Labour Corps from his recruiting station.

In most cases the only record of these postings is a pink form on which is the man's name, the designation 'Labour Corps' or 'Middlesex Regiment', rank (in nearly all cases, private), whether they had served in France before being sent to the Labour Corps, service medals awarded, generally the Victory Medal, and some cryptic notations in letters and numbers.

Mügge's basic pink form shows his 'career' as: Royal Sussex Regiment, Labour Corps and Middlesex Regiment.

Charles Kuhr's form shows him as member of the Middlesex Regiment, listed immediately above two other members, Kur and Kurtz, the latter two not mentioned by Mügge.[31]

Chapter 14

'We Citizens are Proud of You'

F inally having been discharged from the last of several hospitals and with his newly acquired prosthetic limb, Schwarz attended the War Office on 5 August 1921 and made a claim for it to repatriate him to Australia. He confirmed this in a formal letter a few days later, saying he had not been in a position to do so when demobilized (5 May 1920) as 'at that time I ranked as a deserter from the Australian forces.' The WO treated his case as a 'late claim'. Taking into account the king's pardon of 31 July it agreed to send 'Lieutenant W.L. Merritt (né Schwarz) MC late the Royal Fusiliers' home.

When and on what ship he departed the England he had so bravely served, or what he did until he boarded ship for home we do not know.

We next hear of him on his arrival back in Toowoomba on Saturday, 11 February 1922 ...

As the train came to a stop Schwarz glanced through the window of the carriage at the people crowding the platform. He gripped his walking stick, using it for balance as he hauled himself upright. He stayed that way for a long moment, breathing deeply before reaching for his suitcase in the rack above the seat. As he stepped onto the platform a cheer went up and a porter came forward and relieved him of the case. The stationmaster moved to help him. Schwarz waved him away. A moment later his mother and younger sister Minnie emerged from the crowd. The three embraced, their laughter mixing with tears. Schwarz tried to speak, say something, the words caught in his throat.

Schwarz had ridden up from Brisbane, away from the summer heat to the cool highland home he had at times thought he would never see again ...

Among other passengers who left on that morning train was the Federal Attorney General Littleton Groom, whose electoral seat was based on Toowoomba. Groom stood in the background quietly watching the emotional reunion. An old friend, who can be identified only as Bews, approached the trio and said he had been given the honour of driving them to the town hall, where a civic reception awaited. Whether the war hero knew beforehand he was to be formally welcomed we do not know. However, his mother told him at the station she had been asked to attend but had declined. She did not have to tell him the reason why: It was clear she had not forgiven her fellow citizens for the years of torment and humiliation they had inflicted on her. Minnie said she was to represent the family. The town's Congregational minister, the Reverend F.E. Adams, joined them in Bews's car. It was decked out in the Union Jack and Australian flags.

The day was fine and clear. Perfume from the town's gardens, public and private, wafted in a gentle breeze. People stopped on the streets to wave and cheer, Bews responding with a press of the car horn, Schwarz with a polite wave.

At the town hall, Schwarz made his way to the entrance, once again with the help of his stick but without needing human assistance. He was travel-weary. However, he'd been through worse ordeals than what now confronted him and was showing no sign of nerves. People cleared a path, some reaching out to touch him.

Mayor A.R. Godsall greeted Schwarz and escorted him into the main reception room where three long tables stood in a U shape. As the mayor and Schwarz entered, local dignitaries seated at the tables pushed back their chairs, stood and applauded. At the top table Schwarz eased himself into the chair indicated by the mayor. A moment later, Groom appeared, the last of the VIPs to arrive. He'd waited at the station until the crowd had dispersed. He nodded briefly to Schwarz as he took his chair.

Godsall stood, glass in hand, and cleared his throat. 'Gentleman – and ladies – I give you the loyal toast, the king.' Chairs scraped again as the audience found their feet. 'The king,' came the heartfelt chorus. Schwarz had managed to stand, hold his glass, drink and sit again with no apparent effort.

For the next fifty minutes the injured veteran listened quietly to laudatory speeches in which one of the central words of his story was not uttered: 'Deserter'.

Schwarz's version of his story had preceded him thanks in part to the revelatory letter published in the *Toowoomba Chronicle*. In the community generally, its revelations had been accepted with little criticism or analysis. As with many a heroic tale the facts were not going to be allowed to stop the story becoming legend.

Godsall began the orations. He was pleased to see such a representative attendance, including Brigadier General J.C. Robertson who had, until Schwarz's return, been the only local war hero welcomed home with a civic reception. The mayor went on:

> I am sorry that Lieutenant Schwarz's mother is not present to see the way we are honouring her soldier son. But, his sister is present so the family is represented. … Everyone had read little bits of his doings from the time he enlisted in the Australian Army, including the incidents connected therewith until the time he had to leave to re-enlist under a British name, choosing for the purpose the name of our worthy town clerk, 'Merritt'.

His eldest sister, Lily, had married another local Merritt. Like their mother she was a notable absentee from this function. Schwarz did not claim that either the clerk's name or Lily's married name influenced his decision when choosing an alias. In talking of 're-enlistment', the mayor may have believed he was acting the diplomat. Whatever, this was neither the time nor the place for the truth.

Godsall continued in the same obfuscating vein. When Schwarz 'made his position clear to the king, the sovereign was only too ready to pardon him for his change to the British Army.' The mayor's words were greeted with the first of many applauses and no dissent. His expurgation of Schwarz's desertion and false enlistment appears to have stirred the cathartic effect he and his audience were striving for.

The mayor did admit Schwarz had had to go through severe trials on account of his German name. Pointing out the name 'Schwarz' in English meant 'black', he said, had Schwarz gone under that name, he would have been a hero from the word 'go'. Furthermore, many of the leading citizens of the State of Queensland had German names and that did not detract from their worth as citizens or as patriots. He concluded:

> As Mayor and as a native of Toowoomba it gives me great pleasure to welcome Lieutenant Schwarz MC back to his native town. We citizens of Toowoomba are proud of you and we hope that you will be long spared to share the glory that has come to you. You lost a leg at the front and through that and other injuries you had been unable to return to Australia earlier. We were not going to let you return unannounced and I decided to give you this civic reception, and I am very pleased to see so many citizens present to meet you. [Applause.]

As we have seen, although his dismissal from the British Army had influenced Schwarz's decision to return to his hometown, his original preference had been to settle in Britain under his assumed name.

General Robertson next addressed the gathering. He said the civic reception was to honour one of the most worthy of men. Referring to the wartime 'treatment' of members of the Schwarz family in the town, he excused it as the 'over-zealousness of some of the boys and citizens'. As for Schwarz's desertion, he took the mayor's line; he had 'transferred his help to the Imperial Army'. There he had won his commission and the coveted honour of the Military Cross and Bar and been mentioned three times in dispatches. Any soldier knew it was only by acts of the greatest bravery and heroism that these honours could be won. (Applause.) In a further indirect reference to the suffering of Mrs Schwarz, her other children and friends, Robertson said he hoped Lieutenant Schwarz recognized the feeling that had existed was only the result of wartime jealousy and that it must go on during wartime. It was one of the demands of war. During wartime they were out to win the war and they must use every weapon in their power. He felt the City of Toowoomba was behind Lieutenant Schwarz. Its citizens appreciated to the full the struggle he had gone through. He had brought honour to his family, to himself and to his native town. (Applause.) As a high-ranking soldier Robertson must have been aware that the transfer of men between the two armies, Australian and British, was not encouraged from the earliest days of the war by either force. As a policy it was seldom relaxed. By

January 1916, the Australian Government had prohibited all transfers of men who were deemed suitable officer material and Schwarz had shown he was eminently qualified for a commission, other things being equal, which they were not.[1]

The Attorney General (later Sir) Littleton Groom began his address by saying he was unaware he and Schwarz had travelled up from Brisbane on the same train. Groom went on to say that in honouring Schwarz, the people of Toowoomba were honouring themselves as a city. He should have added, forgiving themselves for the fact many of these people had dishonoured Schwarz in word and deed. Groom said the citizens had gathered to express their appreciation of the fine service he rendered his country. (Applause.) 'We also want his worthy mother to feel we are with her in welcoming him back after he has done such honour to her and to his family.' Groom turned his thoughts to the tripartite disarmament talks then underway in Washington and sought disingenuously to draw a parallel between them and Schwarz's heroism. 'The great conference of the world's nations has led them to a new era and we thank Lieutenant Schwarz for the great ideals that promise so much for the world in the years that are to come. We appreciate all the great sacrifices and suffering our wounded men went through, making them all through love of their country.' (Applause.)

Next speaker, Mr Adams, said, as the minister of the church to which Schwarz belonged, he perhaps knew more of the doings of the soldier. 'I am aware he spoke of the anxiety his mother has gone through and although she could not be present I assure you all there is no prouder mother in Australia today than Mrs Schwarz. We trust and pray Providence will watch over Lieutenant Schwarz in the years of civic life that are to come,' he concluded. Adams' claim that Schwarz was a member of his church contradicts the denomination he had nominated on both his AIF and false Royal Fusiliers enlistment papers – Church of England.

The local member of the Queensland Parliament, the Hon. J. Tolme, pointed out he had known 'the lieutenant's grandfather and father, and the grandson is a real Australian as good a citizen as his ancestors.' He referred to Schwarz's 'noble mother', without mentioning the persecution she had suffered. He said she had prayed and hoped during the war, a period that must have been a 'real Garden of Gethsemane'.

The mayor again reached for his glass and proposed a toast to the health of 'Lieutenant Schwarz'.

Once the toast had been drunk and the ensuing applause had died, it was Schwarz's turn to speak. An expectant hush fell over the gathering. What would the hero say? Would he denounce the previous speakers as hypocrites, as men who could not face the truth? Would he reveal the truth of his deception, how and why he had done it – and how he had succeeded? Would he name his helpers and protectors? Would he rail against those citizens who had tormented his family? These and other questions hung in the atmosphere as Schwarz eased his way upright. He spoke, quietly at first. 'I appreciate so much the warm welcome received after so many years of wandering.' (A scattered, tentative applause.) 'I've visited many cities and many towns,' he went on, 'but the place that I am glad to get back to is the town of my birth, Toowoomba.' His voice grew stronger. 'I am very pleased indeed to get back and to make up for any misunderstandings that have been created during the war.' He paused again. Those 'misunderstandings' must have been crowding his mind at that moment. 'I know the majority of people did not believe the silly rumours. I thought they were rather amusing. I would like to say a lot, but cannot. I am so glad to be back.' In his conclusion he expiated himself. 'If I had not gone to the war I would not have considered myself worthy to live in a country like Australia. If anyone is not prepared to sacrifice anything in emergencies like the last, he is not fit to live in that country.' The moment it seemed when he could have spoken out had passed. Schwarz concluded, 'I thank you so much for your welcome.'

His comments, despite their ambiguity, would have been taken by his audience as meaning he had done what he did for Australia. He had not. He fought for a country in which he had no ancestral roots – against a country in which he did. However, none of the dignitaries in the hall that day were about to quibble over distinctions, the words spoken, the mayor's evasions or the general's dismissal of the harassment of the widow Schwarz as an 'over-zealous' reaction of boys and some citizens. The reception had eased both tension and consciences. Eyes had been turned with hope to the future, one in which the world would not be ruled by the might of arms. The warrior who was once a villain had come home – and forgiven his people.[2]

Days after the civic reception, Schwarz called on another veteran and old friend, Ted Harders, in his Toowoomba Motor Company office. Harders was the AIF officer who had almost blown Schwarz's cover when both men were patients in a London general hospital in 1919. Schwarz apologized for lying to him by denying he was Schwarz. Harders recalled years later that he understood Schwarz's reason for hiding his identity – as did others.

On 15 February 1923, G.W. Bennett, the acting deputy commissioner of the Queensland branch of the Commonwealth Department of Repatriation, wrote to the Defence Department's base record office in Melbourne asking for Schwarz's casualty form. Bennett added naively that he understood Schwarz had 'deserted from the AIF'. The reply that came back put Bennett in his place. Schwarz, it said, was not a deserter; he had been 'discharged' from the AIF on 23 October 1915. This was the day he had walked out of the Lydd artillery base.

Mrs Betty Bradley told the author she had never heard Schwarz talk of his wartime experiences. She felt he wanted to enjoy the rest of his life. Her late husband was the nephew of Schwarz's wife. Mrs Bradley recalled Schwarz as tall, athletic and handsome. 'He was solidly built and this caused him problems as prosthetics were not as developed as they are today.' As he aged Schwarz developed osteoarthritis in his left knee and was classified as 90 per cent disabled by the end of his life. Mrs Bradley said, 'I saw him often in later life on crutches, then in a wheelchair.'

Mrs Bradley added that Schwarz was 'a nice man. By that I mean he was a gentleman, kind, caring, with a good sense of humour and a concern for other people.'

As a war hero Schwarz received all sorts of job offers. He tried his hand at real estate and ran a department store before joining the Shell Company of Australia in 1926. Ill health forced him to retire in 1940 from the position of the company's assistant manager of its Queensland branch. An undated, un-named newspaper clipping (circa 1940) found among Schwarz's papers shows he had held the assistant manager's role for the previous five years. The report goes on:

His outstanding ability was soon recognized and after only four years' service he was appointed assistant manager in Western Australia. He returned to Queensland in 1935. During his whole career with the company he has taken a keen interest in the welfare of the staff and it is mainly due to his activities that the Shell Sports and Social Club both here [Queensland] and in WA are in such a flourishing condition. Another marked attribute was his ability to get the best out of those who served under him. His warm and generous nature has endeared him to a host of friends who all wish him and his wife many happy years in his retirement.

The report gives the sanitized version of his wartime ventures:

Leaving Australia with the AIF and subsequently *transferring* [author's italics] to the Imperial Army, he attained commissioned rank in the Royal Fusiliers, was awarded the Military Cross and Bar and was three times mentioned in dispatches. While serving on staff he was severely wounded, resulting in the loss of a leg.

Schwarz was a regular at Anglican church services.

On 4 February 1938 Schwarz married Charlotte (Lottie) Maud Hart at St Thomas's Church, Toowong, Brisbane. It was a late marriage for both. His family says the couple had put off marriage to care for their mothers. Schwarz's mother died in 1942.

There were no children from the marriage. As Captain Penrose had done in those pre-war years with a cadet corps officer, Schwarz mentored a young man, a neighbour's son, Reg Swarz, who went on to become the Federal MP for Darling Downs, the seat once held by Groom. Swarz, who was knighted, had a distinguished parliamentary career serving as Commonwealth Undersecretary for Commerce and holding at various times the ministries of agriculture, repatriation, civil aviation, health and national development. In retirement he was chairman of the Queensland board of the Institute of Directors and on the boards of major companies. He followed Schwarz into the military, gaining his commission in the Citizen Military Force Toowoomba Regiment in 1934. He became colonel of the regiment. During the

Second World War he was a prisoner of the Japanese and was forced to work on the infamous Thailand–Burma Railway.

Schwarz served briefly in the Second World War as a lieutenant in the 1st Australian Garrison Battalion.

The couple had moved to Queensland's Gold Coast in 1940, where Schwarz helped his wife run a boutique. Schwarz died of cancer on 9 January 1969 in Greenslopes Military Hospital, Brisbane, and was cremated following an Anglican service. Through the Australian Repatriation Department Schwarz had received a UK Ministry of Social Security life pension. His 'disablement' was estimated at 90 per cent. The UK Ministry to this day continues to list him thus: 'Merritt, Walter Lancelot, Royal Fusiliers 4233, Royal Fusiliers Second Lieutenant'[3] He had instructed his medals, including his MC and Bar, be sent not to the Australian War Memorial, but to the Royal Fusiliers HQ in London, which was 'very grateful indeed to receive them'.[4]

Schwarz's Petition to King George V

Rokesley Lodge,
95a St George's Road,
BRIGHTON

9 May 1921

To His Majesty the King,

Your Majesty,
I have endeavoured in the enclosed memorandum to tell my story in as few words as possible, and I humbly ask Your Majesty to read it, and if it should please Your Majesty, I shall be very grateful if Your Majesty will grant me Your most gracious pardon, and also grant me permission to use the name under which I fought the Germans.

I have always served Your Majesty faithfully as a private, and as an Officer I honestly believe that I have carried out the terms of the Commission Your Majesty was pleased to grant me.

Although I have lost a limb, I am still capable of bearing arms, and I am quite prepared to lose all my limbs or my life in Your Service.

During the last National Emergency I offered my services to the War Office, and whenever Your Majesty calls for men I shall offer myself.

Hoping that some day I shall again be allowed to serve Your Majesty,
I have the honour to remain,
Your Majesty's most humble servant,
Walter L. Merritt
Lieutenant MC
(né Schwarz)

I, Walter Leslie Schwarz, was born in Toowoomba, Australia, in the year 1896.[1]

My parents were also born in Australia and there is no doubt that my father was of German extraction.[2] He unfortunately died shortly after I was born, but I am certain, that had he lived, he would have trained me, as my mother did, to place my king and country before everything.

The Compulsory Training System was introduced into Australia when I was in my fourteenth year, and I then began to realize my long-cherished ambition, and it was with great joy that I became a cadet of Training Area 11a. I took every advantage of the opportunity offered and after passing through the non-commissioned ranks I studied for and passed the examination for Second Lieutenant.

Captain Penrose, the commanding officer of Training Area 11a, realizing how keen I was on all work of a military nature, gave me a free hand and in addition to lending me many books on military subjects, coached me in map reading and military law, with the result that I passed my examination for lieutenant about three months after obtaining my first commission. During this time I attended many classes of instruction then being held and obtained certificates in map reading, infantry and Army Medical Corps work.

From my fourteenth to my eighteenth year I spent most of my time attending these classes, accompanying the senior officers on staff rides, or drilling the cadets, with the result that a military career attracted me more and more every day.

Early in my eighteenth year, after many conversations with Captain Penrose, I decided to stop playing at soldiers, and join the Regular Army. With this object in view I resigned my commission on 24 June 1914, and as I had no private means with which to enter the Military College.[3] I took the oath of allegiance to His Majesty on that day, and became a gunner in the Royal Garrison Artillery at Fort Lytton,[4] determined to make my way up the ladder until I obtained a regular commission. With this object in view I commenced my new studies, and shortly after enlisting I was appointed an unpaid Acting Bombardier, and although it does not seem very much, it meant a lot to me, as it brought me a step nearer my goal. The life of a gunner at Fort Lytton appealed to me, and I was making good progress owing to my previous training, when on the morning of 5 August 1914 we were awakened by the sound of the alarm, and on falling in we were informed that we were at war with Germany. The remainder of this night and the next few days we spent in preparing the fort for action, during which time we captured an enemy cargo ship.

A few days later news came through of the invasion of Belgium and as I was very keen to go on active service I approached my commanding officer, Captain Weavers, and asked to be sent with the first contingent then being mobilized, either in infantry or artillery. His answer was rather disappointing, for he informed me that none of the Regular Forces would be allowed to go, but in time he hoped that a regular battery would be formed, in which case he would put my name forward.

The prospect of an indefinite wait before I should be allowed to go on active service did not appeal to me, and I was looking for a way out when the fact that my name was of German origin was brought home to me by the receipt of an open postcard bearing the following words: 'When are you going to be naturalized?' This was the first of many such insults I received, and I was continually hearing remarks, obviously directed at me, about 'people with German names, etcetera, etcetera, should not be allowed to serve, as they would probably turn traitors,' or some other equally disgusting remark. These remarks hurt me very much, particularly as I am very patriotic and was very keen to go on active service and do my share of the fighting. Shortly after war was declared I passed my examination for bombardier, and was selected with several other non-commissioned officers to attend a class of instruction for promotion to the rank of sergeant major.

The instructor of this class lost no opportunity of making a joke about my name, which I have no doubt was very amusing to the class, but to me was most unpleasant.

I got through this school and received a temporary appointment as sergeant major, and was detailed for duty with the Australian Expeditionary Forces at Enogerra [*sic*] Camp.[5] I had hoped that on promotion to sergeant major this stupid persecution would cease, but it still followed me, and although I enjoyed the training of the men, I felt that I was always looked upon with suspicion. During the time that I was at Enogerra Camp I made repeated applications to be allowed to accompany the men I was training on active service, either as their sergeant major or as a private, but all these applications were refused, as I was a regular soldier and required for Home Defence.

I had almost given up hope of ever getting away when I received word from Fort Lytton that a battery of regular troops was to be formed and I was asked if I would volunteer. I lost no time in forwarding my application and after the usual medical examination I was passed fit for active service and instructed to return to my unit.

On return to my unit, I automatically reverted to my rank as an unpaid acting bombardier, and in company with other volunteers from Fort Lytton proceeded to the mobilization camp, The Domain, Melbourne. In due course all volunteers arrived from the other forts and we were arranged in sections and as my rank was only acting I was instructed to take my stripe down. This I did, and when a number of promotions were made a little later on I did not receive my old rank, although a number of men were promoted who had not previously held stripes.

I do not profess to know why I was passed over, but it seemed to me that the old persecution on account of my German name was still following me. As I had held a cadet commission, was qualified for the rank of bombardier, and had been a sergeant major instructor to the Expeditionary Force, I could see no other reason than the one just quoted for my treatment.

Shortly after these promotions were made we sailed in the Orsova[6] for England, and I worried but little over my name as I hoped to prove myself in action.

On arrival in England about June 1915, we were stationed at Lydd, Kent. The gun crews, signallers, layers, etcetera, were detailed and we were known as the 55th Battery, 'O' Siege Brigade. Training now commenced in real earnest, and I was detailed with several others to attend a class of instruction for battery commanders' assistants. This course lasted for some weeks, and at the conclusion an examination was held at which I obtained the highest number of marks. I was then detailed for duty with Major Hurst, and at several tests he held he never found fault with my work as a battery commander's assistant.

As all troops were now familiar with their own duty, it was proposed to hold a number of field days, to carry out practice shoots. I had been looking forward to these days for some time when, to my surprise, I was taken off the battery commander's staff and detailed for duty as a mess orderly.

About this time a report was current in camp that no one with a German name would be allowed to accompany the brigade on active service, and as I was Mess Orderly on all occasions when the batteries were on manoeuvres, I came to the conclusion that the reports were correct and that I was being deliberately left out.

Reviewing the situation I determined to seek an interview with my commanding officer, Colonel Coxon [sic] and ask him if my suppositions were correct. This I did on Saturday, 23 October 1915, and after explaining my case to him he informed me that I had better see my battery commander, Major Hurst. I immediately saw Major Hurst and put my case before him. He did not give me any satisfaction and as he gave me evasive answers to my direct questions as to whether my German name had anything to do with it, I decided that my suppositions were correct, and that my services were not required with the 55th Battery, 'O' Siege Brigade.

Having made this decision, I decided to put plans already made into execution, and on the same day, Saturday, 23 October 1915, I absented myself without leave from my regiment and proceeded to London. On arrival at London I registered at the Union Jack Club, and spent the remainder of that day and Sunday, 24 October 1915 in obtaining civilian clothes.

On Monday morning, October 25, I presented myself at Scotland Yard for enlistment as a recruit in the 23rd Royal Fusiliers, the First Sportsman's Battalion, under the name of Walter Lancelot Merritt. The doctor having passed me as fit, I was sworn into the 23rd Royal Fusiliers within forty-eight hours after deserting from my regiment, and it was with the feeling of great relief that I threw off old associations and started afresh under my new name.

In company with other recruits for the 23rd Royal Fusiliers, I was sent to join the battalion at Gidea Park, Romford, and quickly settling down to new conditions, I found myself a paid lance corporal within a very few days.[7]

About 2 December 1915,[8] I was sent on a course of physical drill and bayonet fighting being held at Aldershot, and as I had a good knowledge of this work, owing to my past training, I obtained the highest number of marks in my class and was awarded a good certificate. At the completion of the course I returned to my unit then stationed at Leamington Spa, and commenced making applications to be sent on active service.

While at Leamington Spa, and shortly after my return from Aldershot, I was promoted to the rank of corporal, and after making many applications to my company commander, Captain P. Suckling, and my commanding officer, Colonel Inglis, I was included in a draft, and on approximately 10 March 1916, I joined my battalion the 23rd Royal Fusiliers, 2nd Division, then in France.

I am afraid that my work on that tour was practically nil, for on the morning of 1 May in the trenches near Lens, I was wounded in both arms, Legs [sic] and face. After one or two operations in France I was evacuated to England, and eventually rejoined my reserve unit, the 30th Royal FUSILIERS [sic], then stationed at Olympia, Edinburgh.

On arrival at Edinburgh, I was detailed for duty with the Physical Training Staff, and I have no doubt that I could have remained there for many months but this did not suit me, for although I had been wounded and badly shocked, I had not seen enough active service. I again resorted to my old tactics and after making a number of applications to my commanding officer, Colonel Inglis, I was again included in a draft, and on approximately 24 September 1916, I rejoined the 23rd Royal Fusiliers in the trenches near Hebuterne.[9]

After the usual tour of trench warfare we were relieved and went back on rest. During this rest I was sent for by my commanding officer, Colonel Vernon DSO, who informed me that he had good reports of my first tour with the battalion, and that I was promoted to the rank of sergeant, and was to take charge of a platoon of D Company.[10] This pleased me very much and I wondered whether I should have received any promotion, had I remained with the 55th Battery, 'O' Siege Brigade.

About 2 November 1916 we were moved to the Beaumont Hamel area and took part in that attack on 12 November, after which we held the line for some days.

On or about 20 November we were relieved and sent back on rest. While on this rest I was sent for by my commanding officer, Colonel Vernon, who informed me that he had recommended me for a commission and that I was to proceed to England, to attend an officers' cadet battalion. I am certain that I carried out my duties with the 23rd Royal Fusiliers satisfactorily; otherwise I should not have been recommended for a commission.

I arrived in England about 22 December 1916[11] and was instructed to report at No. 7 Officers Cadet Battalion, Femoy, County Cork, Ireland, on 2 January 1917. I remained at this cadet battalion until 24 April 1917, when I received my second commission as a second lieutenant in His Majesty's Land Forces.

I am certain that Colonel Williams, the commanding officer, and Captain Crofts, my company commander, will testify to my work as a cadet, and at a final interview with Colonel Williams he informed me that I had done well in my examinations, and that he had no hesitation in recommending me for a commission.

In due course I was gazetted to the Royal Fusiliers and on 3 June 1917 I was posted to and joined the 2nd Battalion, Royal Fusiliers, 29th Division, in France.

From Lanches the 29th Division was moved to the Langemark sector, and during an attack on 9 October I was again wounded but remained at duty. When the attacks in this area were completed, the division was relieved, and we went back to rest, and later to practise for an attack, which turned out to be the attack at Cambrai on November 19 1917.

Before going into this attack, I was appointed Battalion Intelligence Officer, and acted throughout the attack and later the defence in that capacity.

For the attacks at Langemark and Cambrai, I believe I was recommended for a decoration, as I received a Divisional Card of Honour signed by Major General Sir Beauvoir de Lisle KCB, DSO. The GOC 86th Infantry Brigade, Brigadier General Cheape CMG, DSO sent for me some few days after this attack, and informed me that I was to come on to his staff as a brigade intelligence officer.

I am certain that the divisional commander of the 29th Division, Major General Sir Beauvoir de Lisle, KCB, DSO and later Major General Cayley, CMG, the BGGS 15th Corps; Brigadier General Knox, CMG, DSO and the brigade commanders of the 29th Division: Brigadier General Cheape, CMG, DSO; Brigadier General Freyberg,

VC, DSO[12] and Brigadier General Jackson CMG, DSO will all testify to my work as brigade intelligence officer. I could also give many more names, including Captain Gee, VC, MC, now a Member of Parliament.[13]

The 29th Division was next engaged in the Lys battle and I received my first honour by being mentioned in Field Marshal Earl Haig's Dispatch, dated 7 April, 1918.[14]

Shortly after the Lys battle the division was engaged in an attack on Ploegsteert, and for my action in that attack I was recommended for the Military Cross, which His Majesty was pleased to approve, the award being published on 2 October 1918,[15] which read as follows:

> T/Sec. Second Lieutenant Walter Lancelot Merritt, 2nd Battalion the Royal Fusiliers. Intelligence Officer. 86th Infantry Brigade Headquarters. For conspicuous gallantry during an attack. At a very critical moment, when one battalion was completely out of touch with both flanks which had been held up, he readjusted the whole line under extremely heavy fire at close range, and led troops into position gaining touch with the advanced battalion and ensuring the safety of its flanks.
>
> Throughout the whole operation his courage and initiative were most marked.

From Ploegsteert the division was moved to the Ypres salient to take part in the Allied offensive on 28 September 1918. This attack was a very great success and as the area to be crossed by the 86th Infantry Brigade was devoid of any landmarks, I carried a large red flag in the centre of the attack, which would be easily seen by the troops on either flank, and by advancing on a compass bearing I was able to bring the troops on to the objective, without losing ground to either flank. From reports afterwards received it was found this flag not only kept the direction of the attacking waves, but enabled the following waves to keep direction.

For my work in this attack I was recommended for a Bar to my Military Cross, which was not awarded, but I received a second mention in Field Marshal Earl Haig's dispatch dated 16 March 1919.

I now come to the final attack I was engaged in, which was east of Ledeghem on 14 October 1918.

The red flag which proved so valuable on 28 September was again called into use, and I again accompanied the attacking wave to assist them in keeping direction. The attack commenced at about 5.30 on the morning of the 14th, and owing to a very heavy mist and the amount of smoke shells used in the barrage, visibility was extremely bad. In company with my observers I followed the barrage and when the visibility improved we found ourselves on the first objective with very few men. The remainder of the brigade had experienced great difficulty in getting through Ledeghem owing to the dense fog, and as we were unable to properly search the ground over which we had advanced, we found ourselves practically surrounded by the enemy. Although we were heavily engaged by the enemy at close range, with machine–gun and trench mortar fire, we succeeded in holding the objective until the brigade arrived.

Shortly after the brigade arrived a number of the enemy opened fire on me at very close range, and succeeded in badly fracturing my right leg. I was evacuated by the Royal Army Medical Corps and on my arrival at No. 5 Base Hospital, Wimereux, my leg was found to be in such a state that to save my life it was amputated above the knee a few days before the Armistice.

While at No. 5 Base Hospital I received word that His Majesty had been pleased to approve the award of a Bar to my Military Cross, and the award, made on 15 February 1919, read as follows:

T/Lieutenant Walter Lancelot Merritt, 2nd Battalion Royal Fusiliers, Intelligence Officer 86th Infantry Brigade Headquarters.

East of Ledeghem on 14 October 1918, as Brigade Intelligence Officer, he carried the directing flag in the centre of the attack and arrived on the first objective with only about forty men, the remainder having got lost in the thick fog and smoke. He and his observers captured twenty-eight of the enemy during the advance, and they held on to the objective until the remainder of the brigade arrived. He was severely wounded in the leg later in the day. He behaved most gallantly and did fine work.

The following extract is taken from a letter I received from my general [Brigadier General G. Cheape] a few days after my amputation:

We are all so awfully sorry to hear that you have lost your leg, but cheer up it is far better to lose a leg than an arm. We got our objectives of the day you were wounded, as we always have in this brigade, thanks to fellows like you.

The following is an extract from a letter dated 4 March 1919 from the late Captain W. Dearden, Brigade Major 86th Infantry Brigade Head Quarters:

I am most awfully sorry to hear that you have got such a rotten wound, and have lost your leg. I hear that you did magnificently, and know you have the Military Cross, and I don't know how many Bars … many, many congratulations, as you deserved all you got.

The following is an extract from a letter dated 15 September 1919 from the French interpreter attached 86th Infantry Brigade HQ:

I sincerely hope someone has kept a record of the speeches made at Christmas 1918, when from General Cheape to the French Froggy, best wishes were sent to two of the finest officers the British Army has had, Captain Dearden and Lieutenant Merritt. We missed you both very much, and I shall always look back to my stay with the staff of the 86th Infantry Brigade.

After a long illness in France, through which I was not expected to recover, I was evacuated to England, and admitted into the 3rd London General Hospital, and later was transferred to the Special Orthopaedic Hospital at Southmead, Bristol. I had several operations at this hospital, and after convalescence at Rock House, Bath, I was admitted into Dover House for the fitting of an artificial limb.

While at this institution I was commanded to appear at Buckingham Palace on 22 April 1920 and had a very great honour of receiving my Military Cross and Bar from the hands of His Majesty.

The following month I was retired from the service on account of wounds received in action and it was with the greatest regret that my career came to such an abrupt ending with only six years' service.

Approximately two of these years were spent in France and in addition to the decorations and mentions already recorded I received a number of divisional honour cards, for my services with the 29th Division.

In conclusion I may truthfully add that on the cessation of hostilities it was my intention to obtain a transfer from a temporary to a regular commission, and with this object in view I put forward an application about November 1917, which was passed by my general and forwarded to Divisional Headquarters.

Failing this I should have enlisted as a private, and made my third effort to gain a commissioned rank.

Appendix II

Fair Play Letter

The Fair Play letter that appeared in the *Toowoomba Chronicle* in 1921 under the following headline: 'What's in a name? Young Toowoomba Soldier Joins a 'Tommy' Regiment and achieves Fame Pardoned by the King'

To the Editor

Sir – Believing the press to be at all times willing and anxious to assist in righting wrongs and insisting that justice shall be done to all irrespective to what nation, creed or class the individual may belong, I now ask you to publish in the columns of your widely read paper the following interesting war record. This is the official military history of a Toowoomba lad for whose arrest a warrant has been in existence since November 1915 for deserting the AIF Forces in England. This young man, Leslie Walter Schwarz [*sic*] by name was born in Toowoomba, and as his name implies was of German extraction. But on the father's side only, his mother's people being Danish. Her family was from Uetersen, Schleiswig-Holstein, formerly part of Denmark, by WWI it was part of Germany. Had his name been other than what it was possibly this story of a grievous error would not have been written, and instead of having to hide his identity and fight under an assumed name in an English battalion his career would have been published far and wide and he would have been hailed as one of Australia's heroes, and deservedly so as his records prove. His poor old widowed mother too was made to suffer and for five long years she had to keep silent and hear her son spoken of as a traitor, spy and everything that was low and contemptible while all the time we knew how nobly he was fighting to uphold the honour of the British race. He deserted from the regiment he was in, yes and by so doing he committed a very serious crime. That is so, but, sir, can you after reading his deposition blame him. I don't think so, I don't want to enlarge on what occurred in camp and from some of his fellow soldiers on the way to England with this exception: While on board the boat and while passing through the tropics, etc., the heat was so great that he like many of his mates fell ill and for a few days was in hospital. Here again he was made to feel an outsider. The nurses, as they passed through the ward would distribute fruit etc., to the men. But for him there was none. It is possible that he may have been mistaken on viewing it in this way. But, sir, on top of all the other insults he received can you wonder at his doing so? However, he bore it all, thinking how soon he would be in France and he would be able to prove to one and all how mistaken they were even though he bore a German name. But it was not to be, as the opportunity was refused him. I am sorry he was forced to do what he did for several reasons, in the first place, a warrant was issued for his arrest, etc., and of course this was spread far and wide, all sorts of impossible stories were told of his doing. He was supposed to have been shot as a traitor at Gallipoli; these sorts of tales were carried to his mother by make-believe sympathizers, and although she denied the story and maintained that her boy was not a traitor the other 'kind' friend, a neighbour, had the audacity to tell Mrs Schwarz that there was a bullet waiting for Les when they got him. This 'kind Christian friend' and patriot had no sons of his own to send to the war. Then came the zealots, who when all honest people were in bed, dropped the live cartridge in Mrs Schwarz's letterbox. Whom did she mean it for – the poor old widow who was praying that God would spare her boy and bring him safely home to her, or did she mean it for the boy who was away fighting for her and making it safe for her so that [she could] snuggle down in her cozy bed and sleep the sleep of the – I was about to say just – but on second thoughts I am not quite certain I would be correct in calling her a just person. Do you think I would be? Then there were others who never knew what it was to be a parent let alone having someone belonging to them over there, busying themselves about this boy … might have understood them but here was a boy reared amongst us and highly respected by all who knew him. Another reason why I am sorry this thing happened is all the honours he has won, and all the splendid work he accomplished was done as an English Tommy and not as a Dinkum Aussie. I do not mean that I grudge the Tommy anything for I know that he deserves all the best we can say of him for amongst them are found as good a men as ever wore shoe leather, still for all that I may be pardoned in saying that I would have liked these records chronicled with and credited to the AIF. I might say that I can produce the Army order wherein his name appears as having won the honours mentioned, also from Army Headquarters giving dates and particulars of wounds received and from the matron and sisters of the hospital in which he was being treated at the time he lost his leg. I received two cables from the matron which says very little hope was entertained of his pulling through as, although his leg was amputated, almost immediately after he was brought in, he had been in no-man's-land for so many hours that his leg had become septic. However, he is now fairly well, but like many another good or brave man, minus a leg. I wanted to move in the matter of clearing his name long ago, having sufficient material in my possession to do so. But he would not consent as he wished to see the thing through. After losing the leg he has had so many operations etc., and being confined to hospital necessitated his waiting till he was well again before acting. He has now done so and the papers submitted to you are duplicate copies of those forwarded to His Majesty and upon which he was judged and awarded a full pardon. I also have the cable which gives me information that the pardon has been granted him. Enclosed herewith are his military records and I tender them in order that his name be cleared of the crimes attributed to him and for that reason only.

(Sgd) FAIR PLAY [no address]

Vitaï Lampada
(They Pass On the Torch of Life)

There's a breathless hush in the Close to-night –
Ten to make and the match to win –
A bumping pitch and a blinding light,
An hour to play and the last man in.
And it's not for the sake of a ribboned coat,
Or the selfish hope of a season's fame,
But his Captain's hand on his shoulder smote –
'Play up! play up! and play the game!'
The sand of the desert is sodden red, –
Red with the wreck of a square that broke; –
The Gatling's jammed and the Colonel dead,
And the regiment blind with dust and smoke.
The river of death has brimmed his banks,
And England's far, and Honour a name,
But the voice of a schoolboy rallies the ranks:
'Play up! play up! and play the game!'
This is the word that year by year,
While in her place the School is set,
Every one of her sons must hear,
And none that hears it dare forget.
This they all with a joyful mind
Bear through life like a torch in flame,
And falling fling to the host behind –
'Play up! play up! and play the game!'

Sir Henry Newbolt (1862-1938)

Written in 1892, *Vitaï Lampada* is Newbolt's best-known poem. It describes how
a schoolboy, a future soldier, learns selfless commitment to duty in cricket matches
in the famous Close at Clifton College, Bristol.

Notes

Chapter 1

1. Letters from German Immigrants in New South Wales, article by George Nadel, Royal Australian Historical Society Journal 39 (part 5), 1953.
2. Scott, Ernest, *Australia During the War,* University of Queensland Press in association with the Australian War Memorial, 1989, p.152.
3. The *Darling Downs Gazette*, 22 July 1858, quoted in Dansie, R.A., 'A Deserving Class of People, Toowoomba's German Heritage,' Queensland Multicultural Co-ordinating Committee publication, 1980, p.1.
4. The Queensland Register of Titles, issued 14 September 1897, copy from Mr David Rohde, Toowoomba.
5. Toowoomba & Darling Downs Family History Society Journal article, vol 17, No. 1 March 2004.
6. Burness, Peter, *Australian Dictionary of Biography*, vol 11, Melbourne University Press, 1988, p.541.
7. The 1885-86 *Ipswich, Toowoomba and Drayton Directory*, Francis Beresford, Brisbane, p.59.
8. The *Toowoomba Chronicle*, 12 March 1863, quoted in 'A Deserving Class,' op. cit. p.12.
9. The *Darling Downs Gazette*, 10 May 1884, quoted in A Deserving Class, pp.63-4.
10. Tampke, Jürgen, *'Ruthless Warfare'*, Southern Highlands Publishers, Canberra, 1988, p.115.
11. *The Commonwealth Year Book 1901-1916*, Commonwealth Bureau of Statistics, Melbourne, p.100.
12. *Australian Encyclopedia*, Collins, Sydney, p.278.
13. Knight, W. Stanley Macbean, *The History of the Great European War*, vol III, The Standard Publishing Company, Melbourne, undated, p.101.
14. Robson, L.L., *The First AIF: A Study of its Recruitment 1914-1918*, Melbourne University Press, 1982, pp.76-7.
15. *The Sun*, 27 August 1969, p.13.

Chapter 2

1. AA471, item no. 311.
2. Cited in Pedersen, P.A., *Monash as Military Commander*, Melbourne University Press, 1985, p.219.

3. Bishop, James, *The Illustrated London News Social History of the First World War,* Angus & Robertson, London, 1982, p.110.
4. Ibid., p.112.
5. Ibid., p.79.
6. Andrews, E. M., *The Anzac Illusion*, Cambridge University Press, 1993, p.184.
7. Ibid., p.185.
8. *The Sydney Morning Herald*, 25 October 1915, p.3.
9. Op. cit., *Anzac Illusion*, p.179.
10. Extract from copy of letter given to author by Jeanette Finlayson.

Chapter 3
1. Foley, Michael, *Hard as Nails: The Sportsmen's Battalion of World War One*, Spellmount, Tonbridge, 2007, p.33.
2. Ibid., p.33.
3. Ibid., p.34.
4. Ibid., p.137.
5. Ibid., p.44.
6. Ibid., pp.50-1.
7. Ibid., p.89.
8. AA-471, item no. 316.
9. BNA WO339/82292, Merritt's service record.
10. Millman, Brock, *Managing Domestic Dissent in First World War Britain*, Frank Cass, London, 2000, p.33.
11. Marrin A, *The Last Crusade: The Church of England in the First World War,* Duke University Press, Durham, North Carolina, 1974, p.139, quoted in Millman, *Domestic Dissent*, p.32.
12. Quoted in Parker, *Peter, The Old Lie: The Great War and the Public-School Ethos*, Constable, London, 1987, p.277.

Chapter 4
1. Department of Defence internment camps, internees, etc. Information for Historians, AWM, Bean Papers, cited in Fischer, Gerhard, *Enemy Aliens*, University of Queensland Press, 1989, p64.
2. Op. cit., *During the War*, pp.137-9.
3. Roetter, Charles, *Psychological Warfare*, Purnell Books, London, 1974, pp.44-7.
4. *Enemy Aliens*, op. cit., pp.124-5.
5. Williams, John, *German Anzacs and the First World War*, UNSW Press, Sydney, 2003, pp.46-7.
6. Op. cit., *During the War*, p.112.
7. Ibid., p.113.
8. 'British-Australasian', 7 March 1918, quoted by McKernan, Michael, *The Australian People and the Great War*, Nelson, Melbourne, 1980, p.167.
9. AA (ACT) CRS A2, item 17/4053, cited in *Enemy Aliens*, p.94.

10. Op. cit., *During the War*, p.145.
11. Based on articles in the *Daily Mirror*, Sydney, Monday, 15 December 1980, p.30, and Tom Fairhall, the *Sun-Herald*, 13 March 1977, p.139. See also, Clarke, Joan, *Dr Max Hertz, Surgeon Extraordinary, The Human Price of Civil and Medical Bigotry in Australia*, Alternative Publishing Co-operative, Sydney, 1976.
12. Op. cit., *During the War*, p.137.
13. Op. cit., *Ruthless*, p.29.
14. Op. cit., *The First AIF*, pp.152-4.
15. Op. cit., *Enemy Aliens*, p. 4.
16. Op. cit., *During the War*, p.144.
17. Heydon, Peter, *Quiet Decision: A Study of George Foster Pearce*, Melbourne University Press, 1965, p.74.
18. Op. cit., *Ruthless*, p.1.
19. Ibid., back cover.
20. Op. cit., *Enemy Aliens*, p.93.
21. Op. cit., *The Australian People and the Great War*, pp.168-70.
22. Ibid.
23. Ibid.
24. *Ruthless*, op. cit., p.90.
25. McGregor, Robert, review article, 'The Electronic Journal of Australian and New Zealand History'.

Chapter 5

1. Op. cit., *Hard as Nails*, pp.126-7.
2. Ibid., p.128.
3. Ibid., p.124.
4. Ibid., p.129.
5. Ibid., p.133.
6. *True World War I Stories*, introduction by John E. Lewis, Robinson Publishing, London, 1997, pp.66-72.
7. *World War I Volume Five, 1915-1916*, Editor-in-Chief Brigadier Peter Young, Marshall Cavendish, New York, 1984, pp.1364-1369.
8. Details from hospital sick list, BNA WO339182292.
9. Professor Joanna Bourke, Professor of History at Birkbeck College and the author of a number of books, including *An Intimate History of Killing*, Granta magazine, 1988, and *The Second World War: A People's History*, Oxford University Press, 2001. Her comments appear under the heading 'Shell Shock during World War One' on the BBC website.
10. Holden, Wendy, *Shell Shock: The Psychological Impact of War*, Channel 4 Books, London, 1998, pp.11-12.
11. Ibid., p.45.
12. Op. cit., *Hard as Nails*, pp.151-2.

Chapter 6
1. Dr R. Brasch, address to the Royal Australian Historical Society, 29 April 1958, RAHS Journal vol 45, part 4, Sydney, 1959.
2. Ibid.
3. Op. cit., *Military Commander*, p.16.
4. Edwards, Cecil, *John Monash*, State Electricity Commission of Victoria, Melbourne, 1970, p.27.
5. Serle, Geoffrey, *John Monash: A Biography*, Melbourne University Press with Monash University, 2002, pp.7-8.
6. Op. cit., *Military Commander*, p.201.
7. Ibid., p.41.
8. Op. cit., *A Biography*, p.202.
9. Op. cit., *Military Commander*, pp.131-2.
10. Op. cit., Brasch address, p.164.
11. Op. cit., *A Biography*, p.206.
12. Op. cit., *Military Commander*, p.131.
13. Ibid., p.215.
14. Andrews, E.M., *The Anzac Illusion*, Cambridge University Press, 1993, p.141.
15. Souter, Gavin, *Lion and Kangaroo*, Fontana, Melbourne, 1976, p.266.
16. Op. cit., Brasch address, p.134.
17. Op. cit., *Lion and Kangaroo*, p.267.
18. Montgomery, Field Marshal (Viscount), *A History of Warfare*, London, 1968, p.494, quoted in *Military Commander*, op. cit., p.294.
19. Op. cit., Brasch address, p.204.
20. Op. cit., *Anzac Illusion*, p.149.
21. Op. cit., *Lion and Kangaroo*, p.268.
22. Quoted in Mügge, Maximilian, *The War Diary of a Square Peg*, Routledge, London, 1920, p.107.
23. Op. ci.t, *The Illustrated London News*, p.58.
24. Ziegler, Philip, *Mountbatten*, Collins, London, 1985, p.36.
25. Op. cit., *The Illustrated London News*, p.58.
26. Arthur, George, *King George V,* Jonathan Cape, London, 1929, p.72.

Chapter 7
1. Winter, Denis, *Death's Men Soldiers of the Great War*, Allen Lane, 1978, p.67.
2. Maltz, Maxwell, *Psycho-cybernetics*, Pocket Books, New York, 1971, pp.3-4.
3. Op. cit., *Death Men's Soldiers*, pp.66-7.
4. BNA WO95/2301.
5. Figures quoted in Terraine, John, *The First World War*, Secker & Warburg, London, 1965, p.155.
6. Macdonald, Lyn, *1914-1918, Voices & Images of the Great War*, Michael Joseph, London, 1988, p.130.
7. Ibid., p.131.
8. Palmer, Alan, Victory 1918, Weidenfeld & Nicolson, London, 1998, pp.256-7.

9. Gillon, Stair, Captain, late King's Own Scottish Borderers, *The Story of the 29th Division – a record of gallant deeds*, Anthony Rowe, Eastbourne, 1925, various extracts.
10. See Appendix 2.
11. Price, Evadne (using the pseudonym Helen Smith), *Not so Quiet, Stepdaughters of War*, Lawrence & Wishart, London, 1987, pp.235-9. First published by Albert E. Marriott, London, 1930. It is seen in some quarters as a reprise of *All Quiet on the Western Front*.

Chapter 8
1. Op. cit., *German Anzacs*, p.149.
2. 'War Hero had to Change Name', *Sunday Telegraph*, Brisbane, 21 April 1985.
3. *German Anzacs*, op. cit., p.139.
4. Dept. of External Affairs, 15 January 1916 (dated 1915). It was stamped 'Received 18 Jan 1916'; held by AA.
5. AA, incorrectly dated 8.9.12.
6. AA, stamped No. 38982.
7. Op. cit., *German Anzacs*, p.139.
8. Ibid., pp.139-40.
9. Ibid., p.140.
10. From family history, supplied to author by daughter, Wendy Jackson.
11. *Toowoomba Chronicle*, undated.
12. Op. cit., *Death's Men*, p.68.
13. Details based on War Office records held by BNA.

Chapter 9
1. Op. cit., *True World War Stories*, pp.252-9.
2. Op. cit., *Not so Quiet*, pp.29-30 & 163. See also Chapter 7.
3. Based on *Toowoomba Chronicle* article, 4 July 1984.
4. *The Times*, Friday, 23 April 1920, p.19, Court Circular.
5. Ramsay Silver, Lynette, *Marcel Caux: A Life Unravelled*, John Wiley & Sons, Australia, 2006.

Chapter 10
1. *Monash, A Biography*, op. cit., p.202.
2. Source: Islington Council Local History Centre.
3. Weightman, Gavin & Humphries, Steven, *The Making of Modern London 1914-1939*, Sidgwick & Jackson, London, 1984, p.122.
4. Association 1914-1918 website. Putkowski's *Shot at Dawn*, 1989, is the standard reference work for soldiers executed under the British Army Act in the First World War.
5. Op. cit., *The First AIF*, p.62.
6. Ibid., p.63.
7. BNA file: WO339182292.

8. Source: Glasgow Corporation Members c.1890-1978, *Glasgow Herald*, 31 July 1944, p.4, obituary under the headline 'Former Town Councillor'. Research: Richard Youngs, Special Collections, the Mitchell Library, Glasgow.

9. BNA document WO339/182292.

10. Op. cit., *Australian Dictionary of Biography*, vol 11, Melbourne University Press, 1988, pp.541-2.

11. AA file. A note dated 28 Feb 1923 from the officer in command of base records Victoria Barracks, Melbourne, to the Department of Repatriation, Brisbane, states: '23.10.15 Discharged in England. Joined Imperial Army'.

12. 3 AWM PR84/134 Schwarz papers.

13. AA file.

14. 'Service History of Walter Lancelot Merritt MC' compiled by Chris Baker, Great War Family Research.

15. AA B2455.

Chapter 11

1. Knight, Christopher & Lomas, Robert, *The Hiram Key: Pharaohs, Freemasons and the Discovery of the Secret Scrolls of Jesus*, Element Books, Boston, 1997, p.344.

2. Ibid.

3. Ibid.

4. Baigent, Michael & Leigh, Richard, *The Temple and the Lodge*, Arcade Publishing, New York, 1989, p.148.

5. *History of Toowoomba Congregational Church 1860-1960*, McDonald & Rosbrook, Toowoomba, undated, p.8.

6. The ministers of the Toowoomba's two Church of England parishes during the period in question were the Reverend W.P. Oakley, St Luke's, who served in the position between 1905 and 1929, and the Reverend A. Davies, St James, 1913-1925. Source: Queensland Anglican synod archives.

7. *Toowoomba Chronicle*, 7 September 1921.

8. Op. cit., *Australian Dictionary of Biography*, pp.541-2.

9. Knight, Stephen, *The Brotherhood*, Panther, London, 1985, p.38.

10. Ibid., p.145-6.

11. The Hiram Key, op. cit., p.355.

12. Paillard, Maurice, *The Three Free-Masons or Evolutional History of Free-Masonry*, self-published, London, 1955, p.11.

13. Ibid., p.14.

14. Jeffers, H. Paul, *History's Greatest Conspiracies*, The Lyons Press, Guilford, Connecticut, 2004, p.187.

15. Op. cit., *Hard as Nails*, p.10.

16. Op. cit., *The Brotherhood*, pp.30-1.

17. Op. cit., *The Hiram Key*, p.326.

18. *Bullfinch's Complete Mythology*, Spring Books, London, 1989, p.309.

Chapter 12
 1. Williams, op. cit., p.6.
 2. Mattner, Max, *The Mattners in Australia 1839-1980*, self-published, p.502.
 3. Correspondence with family members.
 4. Op. cit., *The Mattners in Australia*, p.502.
 5. AA Military Medal Army form W3121, 2 June 1917.
 6. Letter from Colonel Dean to the 18th Battery Club, Adelaide, 1 July 1917.
 7. AA B2455, Army Form W3121. Date of recommendation 16 September 1917. Recommended by Major F.H. Berryman TC (temporary commander) 16th Battery.
 8. Citation without details published in Fifth Supplement No. 30645 of *The London Gazette* dated 19 April 1918 and in *Commonwealth of Australia Gazette* No. 150, 24 September, 1918.
 9. AA B2455, letter dated 24 August 1964.
10. Ibid., 28 August 1964.
11. Correspondence with Mrs Margaret Crisp, eldest child of Edward Mattner.
12. Geoffrey, H., *The Romance of Place Names of South Australia*, author-published, 1986, p.11.
13. From biographical notes written by Edward Mattner's great grand-daughter, Katherine Daniell.
14. Information from Mattner's children, Barbara Hughes and Charles Mattner.
15. Details based on 1968 Parliament of Australia Handbook and Biographical Register, provided by Martin Lumb, Parliamentary Library.
16. Op. cit., Daniell, biographical notes.
17. Colliver, E.J. MC & Richardson, B.H., *The Forty-Third, the story and official history of the 43rd Battalion, AIF*, Rigby Limited, Adelaide, South Australia, 1920, p.10.
18. *Forty-Third*, op. cit., p.219.
19. *Truth*, 22 March 1941, p.10.

Chapter 13
 1. Bourke, Joanna, *Dismembering, the Male Men's Bodies and the Great War*, Reaktion Books, London, 1996, p.149.
 2. Historical Journal, September 2000, p.896.
 3. Op. cit., *Square Peg*, p.75.
 4. Ibid., p.200.
 5. Ibid., pp.12-13.
 6. Ibid., p.13.
 7. Ibid., p.13-14.
 8. Ibid., p.74.
 9. Ibid., p.92.
10. *The Times*, Thursday, 22 March 1917, p.10.
11. Op. cit., *Square Peg*, p.102.
12. Op. cit., *The Times*.

13. Windrow, Martin, *The World War I Tommy*, Franklin Watts, London, 1986, p.4.
14. Op. cit., *Square Peg*, p.75.
15. Ibid., pp.75-6.
16. Ibid., pp.78-9.
17. Ibid., p.88.
18. Ibid., p.83.
19. Ibid., p.85.
20. Ibid.
21. Ibid., pp.113-14.
22. Ibid.
23. Ibid.
24. Ibid., p.187.
25. Ibid.
26. Ibid., pp.194-5.
27. Ibid., pp.198-9.
28. Ibid., p.190.
29. Published 18 Jan 1919.
30. Op. cit., *Square Peg,* preface, pp.v-vi.
31. Source: Ancestry.co.uk.

Chapter 14
1. Bean, C.E.W., *The Official History of Australia in War 1914-1919*, vol III, University of Queensland Press in Association with the Australian War Memorial, fn p.183.
2. This account is based on the *Toowoomba Chronicle* report of the civic reception.
3. BNA website.
4. Letter from Lieutenant Colonel W.W.M. Chard, City of London HQ, the Royal Regiment of Fusiliers, HM Tower of London, EC3, dated 12 February, 1969, to C.M. Schwarz of Lutwyche, Queensland, acknowledging receipt of medals.

Appendix I
1. 17 April 1896, Queensland birth certificate, reg. no. 1896/003426 015728.
2. His father, Heinrich Schwarz was born 'At Sea' in 1859 and later Anglicized his name to Henry. His mother, August Wilhelmina (née Otto), was born in Ipswich, Queensland, in 1866.
3. The Royal Military College, Duntroon, opened in 1911.
4. On the Queensland coast, near the state capital, Brisbane.
5. Correct spelling, Enoggera. The camp is in Brisbane, Queensland.
6. Requisitioned from the Orient Line in April 1915. The 12,000-ton *Orsova* carried Australian reinforcements to Egypt and Europe. She was later in the war used to bring troops from the United States to Europe.
7. Records show the appointment was made on 2 December 1915.

8. Schwarz may have mixed up this date with that on which he was made lance corporal.
9. It was a month before this.
10. This was on 21 September 1916.
11 Actual date, 9 December 1916.
12. Bernard Freyberg was awarded the Victoria Cross and four Distinguished Service Orders for gallantry during the war. He commanded 88th Brigade from January 1918. In the Second World War he commanded the New Zealand forces in Africa and Italy, and was officer commanding one of the corps of Eighth Army. Freyberg subsequently served as New Zealand Governor General in 1946 and was made a baron in 1951.
13. Robert Gee was awarded the Victoria Cross for his part in the Cambrai action in November 1917.
14. Actual date, 28 May 1918.
15. The award was published in *The London Gazette* on 11 January 1919.

Sources

Papers

Key:

AA   Australian Archives
AWM   Australian War Memorial
BNA   British National Archives (formerly the Public Record Office, Kew)

AUSTRALIA

AIF attestation record
AIF record of service
Admission scroll to Toowoomba lodge of United Grand Lodge of Queensland (Freemasons) April 1924.
AWM PR84/134
Commonwealth of Australia Gazette No. 150, 24 September 1918
'Freemasonry Examined' report from the Standing Committee of the Diocese of Sydney, 27 July 1988
Mattner papers: Biographical notes written by Edward Mattner's great grand-daughter Katherine Daniell; 1968 Parliament of Australia Handbook and Biographical Register' provided by Martin Lumb, Parliamentary Library;
Correspondence with Mrs Margaret Crisp, eldest child of Edward Mattner
Letter from Colonel Dean to the 18th Battery Club, Adelaide 1.7.1917
Mentioned in Dispatches citation
Various letters to Mr F.H. Bradley from Australian War Memorial staff: R. Gilchrist, Curator, Private Records, 19 April 1984; David Lance, Curator Audio-Visual Records, 5 November 1984; F.J. Burness, Curator Military Heraldry & Technology, 2 December 1985, 5 February 1986, 26 June 1987
Schwarz's private papers, including Military Cross and Bar citations.
Schwarz Family History' by Joyce Hampson, Toowoomba, contributed by her daughter, Wendy Jackson. Also Jeanette Finlayson article (newspaper and web research Karen Rowe) published in, *Toowoomba & Darling Downs Family History Society Gazette*, vol 17, No. 1 March 2004
Queensland Registrar General: Copy of birth certificate of Walter Schwarz

BRITAIN

A45A: Proceedings of Medical Board (two pages)
Arrival Report
BNA Army Forms:
B2505: Attestation Form (four pages)
B178: Medical History (four pages)
B103: Casualty Form Active Service (two pages)
Correspondence concerning grant of pardon (eighteen pages)
Correspondence re medical condition (11 pages)
Letter from Lieutenant-Colonel, commander 30th Battalion Royal Fusiliers, to War Office.

Letters

From Schwarz (as Merritt) to War Office, 28 July 1919 and 31 August 1919
From Schwarz to War Office re repatriation
Ministry of Social Security Report of Death of Officer, 1969
MT393A: Application for Admission to OCU (four pages)
MT393: Application for Commission (four pages)
Minute sheet
Note from Captain Armstrong RAMC, 100 Field Ambulance, re eyesight test
Notification of relinquishment of commission (two pages)
Précis of claim, and decision
Schwarz's petition to King George for a pardon (seven pages)
SD605: Particulars
Special Collections, the Mitchell Library, Glasgow
The London Gazette, editions 16 May 1917, 11 January 1919, 19 April 1918
Telegram summons to Buckingham Palace for presentation of MC and Bar by King George V.
The 1914-1918 military service history of Walter Lancelot MC, compiled by Chris Baker, Great War Family Research, UK

Articles

'Royal Australian Society Journal' (volume 45 part 4, Sydney, 1959) 'Sir John Monash' by Rabbi Dr. R. Brasch, paper read to society on 29 April, 1958.
'A Deserving Class of People, Toowoomba's German Heritage 1855-1885,' R.A. Dansie (The Queensland Multicultural Co-ordinating Committee (1980).

Newspapers

Daily Mirror, Sydney
Sun-Herald, Sydney

The Sunday Telegraph, Queensland
The Sydney Morning Herald
The Times
The Truth, Adelaide, South Australia
Toowoomba Chronicle

Books

Adam-Smith, Patsy, *The Anzacs*, Nelson, Melbourne, 1985.
Andrews, E. M., *The Anzac Illusion*, Cambridge University Press, 1993.
Australian Dictionary of Biography, vol 11, Melbourne University Press, 1988, pp.177-82.
Beaumont, Joan, *Australia's War 1914-18*, Allen & Unwin, Sydney, 1995.
Beddie, B., ADB online, *Pearce, Sir George Foster (1870-1952.)*.
Beresford, Francis, *Ipswich, Toowoomba and Drayton Directory 1885-86*.
Bishop, James, *The Illustrated London News Social History of the First World War*, Angus & Robertson, London, 1982.
Bullfinch's Complete Mythology, Spring Books, London, 1989.
Commonwealth of Australia Gazette, No. 150, 24 September, 1918.
Commonwealth Year Books, 1926 & 1901-1916.
Edwards, Cecil, *John Monash*, State Electricity Commission of Victoria, Melbourne, 1970.
Fischer, Gerhard, *Enemy Aliens*, University of Queensland Press, 1989.
Foot, Stephen, *Three Lives*, Heinemann, London, 1934.
Gillon, Stair, Captain, late King's Own Scottish Borderers, *The Story of the 29th Division – a record of gallant deeds*, Anthony Rowe, Eastbourne, 1925.
Heydon, Peter, *Quiet Decision: A Study of George Foster Pearce*, Melbourne University Press, 1965.
Holden, Wendy, *Shell Shock: The Psychological Impact of War*, Channel 4 Books, London, 1998.
Jeffers, H. Paul, *History's Greatest Conspiracies*, Lyons Press, Guilford, Connecticut, 2004.
Knight, W., Stanley Macbean, *The History of the Great European War*, vol III, Standard Publishing Company, Melbourne, undated.
Macdonald, Lyn, 1914-1918, *Voices & Images of the Great War*, Michael Joseph, London, 1988.
McKernan, Michael, *The Australian People and the Great War*, Nelson, Melbourne, 1980.
Marriott, R.S., *The Story of Toowoomba's First Hundred Years 1860-1960*, Cranbrook Press, Toowoomba, undated.
Millman, Brock, *Managing Domestic Dissent in First World War Britain*, Frank Cass, London, 2000.
Mügge, Maximilian, *The War Diary of a Square Peg*, Routledge, London, 1920.
Parker, Peter, *The Old Lie, The Great War and the Public-School Ethos*, Constable, London, 1987.

Pedersen, P.A., *Monash as Military Commander*, Melbourne University Press, 1985.

Robson, L.L., *The First AIF: A Study of its Recruitment 1914-1918*, Melbourne University Press, 1982.

Roetter, Charles, *Psychological Warfare*, Purnell Books, London, 1974.

Scott, Ernest, *Australia During the War*, University of Queensland Press in association with the Australian War Memorial, 1989, first published in 1936 as volume XI of *The Official History of Australia in the War*.

Serle, Geoffrey, *John Monash, A Biography*, Melbourne University Press with Monash University, 2002.

Smith, Helen, *Not so Quiet ... Stepdaughters of War*, Lawrence & Wishart, London, 1987, first published by Albert E. Marriott, London, 1930.

Souter, Gavin, *Lion and Kangaroo*, Fontana, Melbourne, 1976.

Tampke, Jürgen, *Ruthless Warfare*, Southern Highlands Publishers, Canberra, 1998.

Terraine John, *The First World War*, Secker & Warburg, London, 1965.

The Forty-Third, the story and official history of the 43rd Battalion, AIF, Rigby Limited, Adelaide, SA, 1920.

The Illustrated Encyclopedia of World War I, Marshal Cavendish, New York, 1984.

The Mattners in Australia 1839-1980, self-published.

Weightman, Gavin & Humphries, Steven, *The Making of Modern London 1914-1939*, Sidgwick & Jackson, London, 1984.

Williams, John, *German Anzacs and the First World War*, UNSW Press, Sydney, 2003.

World War I, vol 5, 1915-1916, Editor-in-Chief Brigadier Peter Young, Marshall Cavendish, New York, 1984.

Index